An Introduction to Criticism

An Introduction to Criticism

Literature / Film / Culture

Michael Ryan

A John Wiley & Sons, Ltd., Publication

This edition first published 2012
© 2012 Michael Ryan

Blackwell Publishing was acquired by John Wiley & Sons in February 2007. Blackwell's publishing program has been merged with Wiley's global Scientific, Technical, and Medical business to form Wiley-Blackwell.

Registered Office
John Wiley & Sons Ltd, The Atrium, Southern Gate, Chichester, West Sussex, PO19 8SQ, UK

Editorial Offices
350 Main Street, Malden, MA 02148-5020, USA
9600 Garsington Road, Oxford, OX4 2DQ, UK
The Atrium, Southern Gate, Chichester, West Sussex, PO19 8SQ, UK

For details of our global editorial offices, for customer services, and for information about how to apply for permission to reuse the copyright material in this book please see our website at www.wiley.com/wiley-blackwell.

The right of Michael Ryan to be identified as the author of this work has been asserted in accordance with the UK Copyright, Designs and Patents Act 1988.

Wiley also publishes its books in a variety of electronic formats. Some content that appears in print may not be available in electronic books.

Designations used by companies to distinguish their products are often claimed as trademarks. All brand names and product names used in this book are trade names, service marks, trademarks or registered trademarks of their respective owners. The publisher is not associated with any product or vendor mentioned in this book. This publication is designed to provide accurate and authoritative information in regard to the subject matter covered. It is sold on the understanding that the publisher is not engaged in rendering professional services. If professional advice or other expert assistance is required, the services of a competent professional should be sought.

Library of Congress Cataloging-in-Publication Data

Ryan, Michael, 1951–
    An introduction to criticism : literature / film / culture / Michael Ryan.
        p.   cm.
    Includes index.
    ISBN 978-1-4051-8283-6 (hardback) – ISBN 978-1-4051-8282-9 (paper)
1. Criticism.   I. Title.
    PN81.L93 2012
    801′.95–dc23
                                            2011035306

A catalogue record for this book is available from the British Library.

Set in 10.5/13pt Minion by SPi Publisher Services, Pondicherry, India
Printed in Singapore by Ho Printing Singapore Pte Ltd

1   2012

For Nathaniel

Contents

Preface

An Introduction to Critical Analysis

Criticism is the analysis of human cultural life. What science does to physical life criticism does to cultural life. It takes it apart and studies it and figures out why it works the way it does.

Such analysis ranges from the techniques used to make cultural artifacts such as novels, movies, music, and paintings to the ideas contained in such artifacts, the world out of which they arise, and their implications in our lives.

The specific region of culture that criticism analyzes is stitched into a larger cultural web that includes money, language, mathematics, engineering, commerce, digital computing, religion, and law. Without such culture in the larger sense, there would be no human life on earth. It is our most important creation as humans. It allows us to manipulate things without laying our hands on them, and it allows us to make the world work by using symbols or signs such as currency and words rather than hammers and levers.

The region of human culture that criticism addresses, the culture of plays, movies, novels, poems, public discourse, and songs, has an important function within that larger culture. It directs human thought, feeling, and belief in ways that help maintain human physical existence. It reinforces norms that guide behavior, and it remakes old assumptions about how we should behave that have lost their adaptive usefulness. Cultural artifacts promote ideas that motivate action and they provide moral instruction. They are teachers, ministers, advertisers, politicians, and parents all in one. They help us manage our lives by providing us with useful examples of how to live. Culture in this sense is akin to biochemistry. It does not do the actual work of life, but without the instructions it provides, that work could not occur.

The arts, including poems, novels, and plays, were invented at the same moment in human history as large-scale communities because the arts spread norms, and norms ensured that we humans could live together cooperatively. They allowed us to transcend our animal nature, which mandates violence and mutual predation for the sake of survival. To get beyond that stage of human existence, humans had to develop new cognitive powers, and one of the crucial powers was the ability to hold ideas and images in one's mind independently of things we perceive in the world. That kind of thinking ability led to the invention of religion; it made writing possible (seeing ideas in marks on a page); and it worked to invent laws based on ideal principles of justice. It also made norms possible, unwritten rules that were passed on through speech of various kinds such as oral tales and plays, as well as religious teaching and school instruction. Another name for the new cognitive ability that made cooperative civilized communities possible is imagination.

Cooperation is essential to human civilization because it makes larger human communities possible. Those communities were first enabled by changes in human cognition that made it possible for humans to use signs and to infuse objects with ideas. Strokes on paper became numbers that facilitated trade; signs in the marketplace became laws that were instructions for living properly; and certain ritual acts became embodiments of a regulating principle in human life – "God's commandments" – that made people behave in ways useful to the survival of the community.

With what we call "meaning" – the association of ideas with things – was born the human ability to create large-scale civilizations. Large-scale human communities could only exist if all people held the same ideas of right and wrong in their minds. And religion, which might be called the first major human art form, provided such unanimity. It consisted of a mix of theater, fictional narrative, painting, and song. With time, actual theater supplanted it, and with even more time, modern cultural forms such as novels and movies took over the task of providing positive images of norms distinguishing right from wrong that sustain cooperative human communities still. *The Great Gatsby* teaches, among other things, that excess wealth is dangerous and destructive of human relations. It promotes a norm of moderate behavior.

As human civilization has developed over the past several millennia, culture has moved from unanimous meanings and beliefs that were largely religious in character to meanings that are multiple, complex, and contingent. Culture has become a realm where norms are debated as much as promoted. Societies held together by one religion are increasingly supplanted by ones in which multiple stories contend regarding what is true and good. As a result, the critical analysis of culture requires a variety of critical approaches. You will encounter them in this book.

1

Formalism

Major Texts

Viktor Shklovsky, "Art as Technique"
Vladimir Propp, *Morphology of the Folk-Tale*
Mikhail Bakhtin, *Discourse in the Novel*
Cleanth Brooks, *The Well-Wrought Urn*

Major Ideas

- Formalists pay attention to the "how" in "how things are done." They notice form. When a ballerina executes the familiar moves of the dances in *Swan Lake*, she performs the story of the ballet, but she also performs moves that are technical in nature; she follows certain well-known forms. Those watching might be struck by what good form the ballerina has or by how well she executes moves they know so well, quite apart from the content of the story of the ballet. Form in this example would consist of "the way something is done" as opposed to "what it is about" or "the story being told."

- The story of the ballet would not be possible without the dances that construct the story, the forms the ballerina uses or performs. If you removed the dances and sat in the theater watching the stage, there would be no story and no *Swan Lake*. Form in this broad sense means the practical dimension of art, the way it is executed and constructed so that it

An Introduction to Criticism: Literature / Film / Culture, First Edition. Michael Ryan.
© 2012 Michael Ryan. Published 2012 by Blackwell Publishing Ltd.

can tell stories or make meanings. Some would say that form in this sense is all that art is. The narrative reality of *Swan Lake* on the stage consists of practical exercises in balletic form. You may think you are seeing a story, but in fact all you are seeing is performers executing techniques.

- If content is not possible without form, form is also radically separable from content, the things stories are about. Think of a ballerina in the practice room going through the moves that she will be performing that evening in the actual ballet. They are the same as those in the ballet, but they are without significance. They are forms only, mere exercises in technique. In this sense, form is pure technique or technique without any content attached to it. The study of this practical dimension of a work of art constitutes Formalist Criticism.

- The Russian Formalists argued that the language of literature should be studied in and of itself, without reference to meaning. For example, the way stories are told (the "narrative") is an important dimension of fiction. Certain writers are more known for the way they tell stories than for the ideas they advance. James Joyce is famous for his "stream of conscious-ness" technique, for example, in his epic novel *Ulysses*. Marcel Proust, in *Remembrance of Things Past*, engages in a meditation on the role of time in human life by telling his entire novel retrospectively, beginning in the distant past and ending in the present. Technique and form are crucial to poetry. Some forms were prescribed, such as the sonnet, but more recent poetry is free-form. In poetry, such techniques as rhyme and repetition distinguish poetic form from other literary forms such as prose.

- Another group of Formalist critics, the American New Critics, felt literature embodied universal truth in concrete form. They were more concerned with how literature made meaning than with how techniques could be studied entirely on their own apart from what they meant. Often the meanings these Formalist critics were interested in were reli-gious paradoxes – such as one loses mortal life but gains eternal life. They also felt "great" poems were complex, made up of elements in ironic tension with one another – a universal idea and a concrete image, for example. Irony means that two very different things are said in the same statement, and the New Critics felt that great complex poetry was ironic for this reason. It is universal and particular, ideal and concrete, idea and image all at once. Moreover, if one studies a poem, one usually finds that it is an organic unity: the form of the poem and the ideas it communicates are inseparable. Form is usually a perfect embodiment of theme in great poetry. The "what" of literature is usually bound up quite tightly with the "how" of literature. For example, William Wordsworth felt life was paradoxical; the simplest natural things tend, according to him, to embody universal truths. And his poems rely quite heavily on paradox.

Major Terms

Form/Content Form is how a work of art is done or made, the techniques and procedures that an artist uses to construct a story or convey a feeling or an idea. Content is what a work of art is about.

Technique A technique is a particular way of doing something such as telling a story or establishing a setting or constructing a character. Techniques are also called devices and procedures.

Narration/Story The narration or fabula is the series of events that are actually reported or represented in a novel or a film. The story or *szujhet* (or subject matter) is the much longer span of time and of life from which the events reported, represented, or narrated are selected. It is the story world itself, rather than the story about that world. Another term for story is "diegesis."

Perspective/Point of View Perspective is the position from which a narration operates. A film like *Iron Man* is told from the point of view or perspective of a wealthy western white man. Predictably, the way people very different from him – angry Middle Easterners, for example – are portrayed is skewed by that perspective; they appear menacing because they are so different; his perspective is laden with fear and he paints the world accordingly. Other terms associated with perspective are "focus" and "focalization."

Motif A recurring element of a narration such as a particular event or a particular symbol or metaphor used repeatedly.

Function Narratives often follow patterns that they share with other narratives. In folk-tales, a common function is "the hero leaves home." All tales seemed to have this particular narrative turn.

Discourse A coherent body of statements about something such as an event, an object, or an issue – for example, the discourse on race or the discourse of science. A discourse is generated by rules for making statements that produce consistency and uniformity across different statements. Such norms make for unity or consistency across different statements. They also make for easily demarcated boundaries between statements internal to the discourse and statements that fall outside its range.

Genre   A group of artistic works that share certain traits. Works within the genre are easily recognized as being similar to one another and as being examples of the genre's rules or conventions (agreements to do something a certain way). For example, works in the genre of melodrama usually contain a theme of unjust action wronging someone, who must vindicate his or her virtue.

Hypotaxis and Parataxis   These terms describe two different ways in which relationships between successive ideas are expressed. In parataxis, the main elements are placed in a sequence of simple phrases, linked together by the conjunction *and* (or variations such as *but*). In hypotaxis, relations are specified as subordinate clauses joined by temporal or relational links such as *when, although, after,* etc. The Old Testament largely uses parataxis, but many modern translations use hypotaxis extensively, as it is seen by modern readers as providing more interest and variety. However, the narrative pace is changed by doing this, and certain deliberate breaks in the pattern are obscured. An (invented) example of the same idea, rendered in the two different styles is: "When Joseph arrived at the field, he spoke to his brothers, urging them to come home even though they were unwilling," and "Joseph arrived at the field and spoke to his brothers and said 'come home' but they would not."

Poetic Meter   Traditional metric poetry uses five rhythms of stressed and unstressed syllables. An iambic foot of verse is unstressed/stressed: "That *time* of *year* thou *mayst* in *me* be*hold*." A trochaic foot is stressed/unstressed: "*Tell* me *not* in *mourn*ful *num*bers." A spondaic foot is stressed/stressed: "*Break, break, break* / On thy *cold gray stones*, O Sea!" Lines vary in number of feet. The iambic pentameter consists of five iambic feet as in the example above. Tetrameter has four feet, trimeter three, and hexameter six.

New Criticism   The approach to literature advocated by a group of critics in the middle of the 20th century in America. Alan Tate, Cleanth Brooks, Robert Penn Warren, and others argued that literary study should focus only on the text – not on history, psychology, or sociology. The goal was to describe the organic unity of the work, the way form and content cohered perfectly. An author's intention was irrelevant, as was a reader's reaction. Only the text, especially the intricate web of image and argument, was worthy of "close reading." The New Critics were therefore skeptical of the notion that a writer's intention determined what a work meant (the "intentional fallacy"), and they opposed criticism that relied on a reader's emotional reaction to or impression of a work (the "affective fallacy").

Summary and Discussion

How you do something is sometimes more important than what you do. If you walk into a job interview with an arrogant swagger dressed as if you just got out of bed and sit slouched picking your nose and daydreaming while the interviewer poses questions, you in all likelihood will do less well, despite being eminently well qualified for the position, than if you adopted a more professional demeanor, dressed in a suit, adhered to the rules of proper manners, and listened attentively while sitting up straight. Good posture can be everything. It is a species of what is called "good form," which means "playing by the rules" or "following the reigning conventions of behavior."

Similarly, how you say something can be as important as what you say. You can say "I love you" softly and gently, and it will mean one thing – a sincere expression of affection and commitment – or you can say it with the emphasis falling heavily on "you" followed by a questioning rise in tone – as in "I love YOU? (of all people)." The tone is now sarcastic rather than sincere, and the meaning changes as a result from sincere affection to something like "You've got to be kidding." The feelings your statement generates will be quite different.

Formalists attend to these differences in how things are said or done. All works of culture – film, poem, rap song, novel – consist of technical choices that have meaning. You may have an idea – "adultery is really not a vice; it can be an expression of genuine, even divine love" – but getting it across in a work of fiction requires that you use literary techniques to create character, plot, situation, and event. You have to use words, wrought in a certain way, to make meaning. Or you have to choose where to place your camera, what lighting to use, how to direct actors to deliver lines, and so on.

Formalist critics notice that "how" is often as important as, or more important than, "what." We like to think books and movies and songs are about life. And they are, of course. But they are also technical exercises that entail choices regarding such things as the perspective from which the story will be told, the kind of tone used, the logical evolution of the narrative, the way characters are constructed, the way lyrics are chosen and arranged, the structure of the melody, the placement of the camera, the kind of lighting used, the images chosen to illustrate points, and the like.

In order to mean, cultural works must have a formal dimension that consists of carefully chosen and arranged techniques.

Formalists in literary study were initially concerned primarily with poetry because poetry is so different from ordinary speech. It is clearly formed, made different by being arranged differently. It possesses rhythm and rhyme; it has melody and depends often on phonic harmony created by alliteration or the repetition of sounds. "Poetics" is the term for the formal study of poetry.

The formal analysis of a poem begins with a simple non-judgmental and non-interpretive description of the work. It describes the themes, the setting, the speaker or narrator, the characters if any, the implied world of the poem (what precedes the poem and what follows), the structure of the poem, such as the breakdown into stanzas, the genre or type of poem, the meter used (such as iambic pentameter), the rhyme scheme, the emotional movement of the poem toward a climax if any, the repetition of words, the images used, the figurative language such as metaphors and symbols, the congruence or dissonance of sounds in alliteration and assonance, the overall thematic argument as that is worked out in the language, etc.

Here are websites that will provide you with most of the important terms to use in such a basic description: http://www.infoplease.com/spot/pmglossary1.html; http://www.factmonster.com/ipka/A0903237.html.

Formalists are also concerned with rhetoric, the shape a writer gives to thoughts or themes in various language constructions. Rhetoric consists of more complex forms of speech or writing that writers use. For example, a favorite rhetorical form American New Critical Formalists studied was paradox (as in the Shakespeare line "Reason in madness"). Another was irony, as when Orson Welles juxtaposes an image of Charlie Kane feeling triumphant with an image of him reflected in glass and looking quite insubstantial and ephemeral. If paradox brings opposed ideas together, irony undermines one proposition with another. It consists of saying one thing and meaning something quite different (as when someone says "You look lovely, darling," when in fact you just got out of bed). Irony is also found in theater and film, when a situation is such that the audience knows more than one of the characters. Irony of situation occurs when a result is quite different from what was intended (e.g., an attempt to save a life ends a life).

For a list of rhetorical terms used in such analysis, here is another site: http://www.tnellen.com/cybereng/lit_terms/.

American New Critical Formalists like Cleanth Brooks (*The Well-Wrought Urn*) were concerned with how poems embody universal truth. Poems contain concrete images that are just the opposite of universal truths, which are abstract rather than concrete. Brooks believed all poetry, therefore, was paradoxical because it was both universal and specific at the same time. He favored a religious view of poetry that saw it as the embodiment of spiritual meaning (universal truth) in concrete figural form (the poem).

Examples of Formalist Critical Analysis

A good example of a poem that clearly embodies what New Critic Cleanth Brooks contends is Williams Wordsworth's "Intimations Ode" (http://www.bartleby.com/101/536.html).

It is organized around a paradox: all that we cherish passes, yet it passes away only in order to last forever. It is still possible to find something permanent and enduring in nature, and that is spirit. Spirit guarantees a more enduring life than the one of physical experience that is so fleeting and that passes so quickly. In a way, although we lose, we gain. That is the paradox of nature in as much as it embodies an enduring, transcendental spirit.

The kind of spiritualist thinking one finds in Wordsworth and Brooks has been increasingly displaced in recent decades by more scientific ways of thinking. Now it is more common to believe that there is no spirit world. The physical world is all we have. Many writers in this post-religious tradition have written poems about the change from spiritualism to a more physicalist vision of life. Increasingly, they are skeptical of the idea that there are "universal truths," spiritual ideas that apply to everyone everywhere and that are a version of Christian theology. One of the more formally interesting is Elizabeth Bishop. Her poem, "At the Fishhouses" is about the fact that the emblems of Christian religious belief persist, yet the spiritual world they supposedly embody no longer seems credible (http://www.poemhunter.com/poem/at-the-fishhouses/).

The structure of the poem seems to invite a meditation on the possibility of a spiritual world. The first stanza is about physical things; the second, the very short one, seems a deliberate hinge in that it talks of the water's "edge," and the third meditates on religious ideas. It is as if Bishop were trying to be Wordsworth – looking at the physical world and then finding in it emblems of "immortality," a spirit world behind the physical one. But the poem seems more about how difficult and exciting it is to live in a world that can no longer be said to contain a Christian version of spirit. For Bishop, the world is all there is.

Notice how the first stanza contains descriptions of physical objects with resonance in Christian imagery – the wooden captan shaped like a cross, the dried blood that recalls the crucifixion of Jesus Christ, the central story of the Christian religion, and the fisherman who recalls the Christian idea of the "fisher of men" who would bring those without faith into the Christian faith. Christ is often figured as a fish ("ichthys") because that was an ancient symbol of the way the spiritual and the physical world joined together. But notice that Bishop is less concerned with suggesting that there is a spiritual meaning in these physical objects than with noting how they are, as objects, simply beautiful in themselves. She seems to suggest that the process of physical life is sufficient. We should concentrate on it, like the old fisherman, and not try to find spirit where there is none.

Notice that the net is "almost invisible," which suggests the way, in a spiritualist vision of existence, the physical world would disappear into its true meaning as an embodiment of spirit. But the physical world persists in Bishop's vision, and it assaults the senses: the codfish make her nose run and her eyes water. Moreover, while the church-like fishhouses with their high peaks evoke the possibility of transcendence (of leaving the physical world for the spiritual by moving up the gangplank at the hinge between water and land), this possibility is countered by the sheer weight of the sea, a dense physical object that seems resistant to being seen as an embodiment of spirit. It is "opaque," rather than being a transparent glass through which one might, as one would in a Wordsworth poem, see Eternity. "Translucence" rather than "transcendence" seems to be what occupies Bishop, and that word is used to describe the simple physical beauty of the actual world. Perhaps this world is enough, she seems to suggest. Perhaps we need to reach or imagine no further by turning it into an embodiment of spirit. While the Christian cross-like wooden capstan is "melancholy," the old man himself, for example, possesses "the principal beauty." He is committed to life itself, lived through the repetition of simple tasks that are "unnumbered." They never turn into spirit; they simply endure and continue, taking hope from Lucky Strikes, an image of the way a brave person who has given up the security of religion might face life in the physical world.

Bishop begins to speak in a Wordsworthian spiritualist way twice and then interrupts herself and returns to the physical world. Twice she begins to intone "Cold dark and deep ..." It is as if she were a poet like Wordsworth who sees the physical world as having a "deep" meaning that is the universal truth of the spirit world that is "bearable to no mortal," but she stops herself, allows herself to be interrupted by everyday things like a seal. The physical world has small pleasures, not big transcendental rewards, she seems to suggest. But it is also a hard place, and enduring life in it without a sense of spiritual meaning can be difficult. Bishop suggests we may be protecting ourselves from facing the hard truth of physical reality – that we all die and pass away. That is why she recalls the hymn "A Mighty Fortress Is Our God." The fantasy of God protects us from the hard reality of the world. Knowledge of that reality burns your tongue; it is cold and hard; and unlike the fixed meanings of the Christmas trees and the churches, it is in physical time and flows on and away constantly: "our knowledge is historical, flowing and flown." Christmas trees are only natural objects; it is we who turn them into spiritual meaning. But by themselves they are simply innumerable things. They make the physical world special, but that world, for Bishop, is indifferent. It recognizes none of our special occasions, our ways of making meaning of it. The Christmas trees "stand/waiting for Christmas," as the cold water of the world swings "indifferently ... above the stones." Fire is often used in the Christian tradition as an image for the transmutation of physical things into spiritual ones. But Bishop's physical reality is one that cannot be burned away into spirit ("transmutation of fire"). Its flame is oddly "gray," and it "feeds on stones," things that cannot be burned. In her metaphor, they resist being transmuted into spirit.

Bishop's technique in the poem consists of creating resonances with Christianity through allusions ("A Mighty Fortress," the bloody capstan). But while Wordsworth turns the ordinary world into a manifestation of spirit, Bishop evokes that poetic gesture and then does not perform it. She remains resolutely on the surface of the ordinary.

The Formalist study of fiction is called narratology because it is often concerned with how stories are told. Consider the formal difference between James Joyce in *Ulysses* and Ernest Hemingway in *In Our Time*, books written just a few years apart. Hemingway's theme is toughness and how to get it. Men who fail are losers. Those who succeed harden themselves against the world and hold emotional attachments at a safe distance. They keep a tight lid on their emotions.

What kind of form would you expect with these themes? Here is an excerpt from a story about a young man fishing in a river near a swamp:

> A big cedar slanted all the way across the stream. Beyond that the river went into the swamp. Nick did not want to go in there now. He felt a reaction against deep wading with the water deepening up under his armpits, to hook big trout in places impossible to land them. ... In the swamp fishing was

a tragic adventure. Nick did not want it. He did not want to go down the stream any further today. He took out his knife, opened it and stuck it in the log. Then he pulled up the sack, reached into it and brought out one of the trout. Holding him near the tail, hard to hold, alive in his hand, he whacked him against the log. The trout quivered, rigid. Nick laid him on the log in the shade and broke the neck of the other fish the same way. He laid them side by side on the log. They were fine trout.

Notice the simplicity of the sentences, the clean sense of orderliness in the prose. No feminine swirls here, no decorative adjectives. No signs of what other men looking on might take to be emotionality or vulnerability. Notice too the symbolic lay-out of the landscape, with the wet swamp that threatens to swallow up the man on the one side and the neat log on the other where the man can do his brutal work and maintain a sense of order in the face of potential engulfment and tragedy or loss. The simple form of the sentences is a way of keeping what the swamp represents – loss of clear boundaries around oneself – at bay. "Nick did not want it" is a way of ensuring through the very clean, clear, crisp, unadorned form of the sentence that he will not be overwhelmed by the swamp. Form here is almost a weapon like the knife. Its sharp edge keeps the male keen and out of the swamp of emotional disclosure and self-loss.

Now consider Joyce who concludes *Ulysses* by occupying the perspective of a woman who has just had an adulterous relationship during the day and who now lies in bed beside her husband, an affable, not at all duped, keenly aware man who nevertheless puts up with her antics. Here she thinks about a past flirtation, a play about adultery, the onset of menstruation, and her lover of the afternoon:

"I was fit to be tied though I wouldn't give in with that gentleman of fashion staring down at me with his glasses and him the other side of me talking about Spinoza and his soul that's dead I suppose millions of years ago I smiled the best I could all in a swamp leaning forward as if I was interested having to sit it out then to the last tag I wont forget that wife of Scarli in a hurry supposed to be a fast play about adultery that idiot in the gallery hissing the woman adulteress he shouted I suppose he went and had a woman in the next lane running round all the back ways after to make up for it I wish he had what I had then hed boo I bet the cat itself is better off than us have we too much blood up in us or what O patience above its pouring out of me like the sea anyhow he didn't make pregnant as big as he is."

The first thing that strikes one about the form of this passage is the lack of grammatical markers; everything flows together. Molly is funny, warm, earthy, resentful, and quite physical. She thinks more about getting laid well than about whether or not she is a proper woman or has a proper feminine identity (whatever that might be). The tone is one of good-humored tolerance, especially toward things normally considered "sins" by her Catholic compatriots in Ireland at the beginning of the 20th century. That tolerance suggests an emotional lability and openness that does not need to prove itself through evidence of order, firm boundaries, or toughness. Quite the opposite, in fact.

Form is often appropriate to content. It is the mode of execution of certain ideas or themes. In the case of Hemingway, the form of the sentences is crisp and clear, simple and neat, like the orderly boundary Nick wishes to maintain in the face of the symbolically feminine swamp. In the case of Joyce, the form of the sentences is fluid and boundaryless, associative and connective, like the personality of Molly Bloom.

Narrative is the ordering of events in a story or film such that they plausibly resemble real life. In some respects, narrative emerges from perspective. To see the world from a particular perspective is to tell the story of the world in a particular way. Perspective allows you to see only so much of the world. Narratives are therefore always focalized; they allow one to see, but they limit what one sees.

Narratives are selective constructs. When we tell a story about what happened to us the night before, we do not recount every second and every single thought we had. We instead select and recount only those events and thoughts that are most relevant, most significant, or most interesting for the effect we wish to create. All fictional stories and all films do the same thing. They select from actual events and combine the selected material into a sequence called a narrative.

Narratives are exercises in logic. Each event is a cause from which follow subsequent events. Narratives are also usually spatial as well as temporal. They tell stories in sequence through time, of course, but they also embody spatial schemes of meaning. *The Scarlet Letter* poses an ideal of natural freedom against a social world in which religion and law are fused for the sake of moral government. That spatial structure of meaning is worked out through the temporal narrative.

Narratives are characterized by motifs and functions. A motif is a recurring element within the same story – say, a reference to a blind man's cane in Joyce's *Ulysses*, for example. A function is a recurring element found in a diverse array of stories. In all heroic narratives, for example, the hero leaves home, is tested, receives help, and vanquishes the villain. The author draws on such forms or patterns in making his or her particular story. As a result, the story contains elements that can be found in other similar stories. Its form is shaped by conventions or formulaic patterns specific to its particular genre (the melodrama, the heroic legend, the comedy, etc.). The conventions of genre lend shape to certain kinds of stories such as the comedy and the tragedy. In comedy, the hero is usually low on the social scale and rises up; in tragedy, a figure who is high up socially falls. Certain such conventions are specific to historical eras. We seldom read or see tragedies these days because the era of kings and nobles is past. We see lots of comedies, on the other hand, because we live in a class-stratified society in which rising up socially or economically is a constant issue, one that provides many examples suited to comedic purposes. *Knocked Up* is a comedy of class ascent; a poor boy gets a well-to-do girl. His virtue transcends the usual barriers to non-success. Comedy is an appropriate form for such content because comedy thrives on breached boundaries and broken rules. And the main male character breaches a class boundary in the story of the movie.

Let's now consider a specific example of narrative at greater length. *The Scarlet Letter* is about a minister who gets a young woman pregnant and then refuses for years to take public responsibility for what he has done. He allows her to suffer the opprobrium of the community and to be branded with the red "A" for adulteress. She is stigmatized and lives a life of shame – at first. She eventually, through her good works, wins over the community, who come to see her first as "Able", then as "Angel." The minister eventually reveals his sin and dies from his private suffering, but not before he publicly adopts his illicit family and acknowledges paternity of the child.

The Scarlet Letter is a symbolic narrative in which characters represent certain types – typical emblems of particular kinds of strength or virtue or vice. Hester is a woman associated with nature and with a supposedly (for the era) natural woman's role of care-giver and nurturer. But she is also a free spirit who defies the authority of the world she lives in. Her daughter Pearl represents embodied spirituality in nature, a spontaneous being whose every act is an expression of virtue. Chillingworth represents moral supervision that would torment those guilty of natural lapses such as adultery, while Dimmesdale is the emblem of all the damage such moral government does in the world by making nature seem evil.

The novel's form is also ironic. It begins with one set of moral premises, but during the course of the narrative those premises are inverted. The term for this is chiasmus, or crossing. In the course of the narrative, terms cross and change value. What began as virtue ends up seeming like vice, and what began as vice appears in the end to be the only true virtue. At issue is the 19th-century religious notion of "sin," the idea that natural human actions can be categorized as evil by those who disapprove of them. Hawthorne demonstrates that what the Puritan church authorities declare to be sin – sexual desire – is in fact a universal human trait. Both Hester and Dimmesdale, the two putative sinners in the Puritan moral scheme, sense others around them who share their passionate sexuality.

The novel is filled with symbols and metaphors largely because, while writing it, Nathaniel Hawthorne read a controversial book that appeared the same year called *God in Christ* by Horace Bushnell, a Protestant theologian and minister who was persecuted for his beliefs, a theme that Hawthorne takes up in his novel. Bushnell devotes his first chapter to "typology," the idea that divinity manifests itself in emblems in the world. For Bushnell, as for Hawthorne in the novel, sunlight is a symbol or emblem of divinity. The scarlet A that Hester is obliged to wear as a sign of adultery is an important symbol largely because, for Hawthorne, it comes to mean something quite different from what the Puritan clerics intended. It is a sign of Hester's natural spirituality because she has made it in such an ornate and creative way that it subverts the harsh simplicity and simple-mindedness of the Puritan moral scheme. Her private spirituality is beyond the reach of conservative moral government. It is its own justification. The Puritans taught children using a simple "primer" that associated letters with words and moral lessons ("In Adam's fall, we sinned all"). Hawthorne in the novel favors instead a more naturalist brand of religiosity that sees divinity in nature. Hester's free-spirited reworking of the A, so that it symbolizes natural talent and natural moral freedom, subverts the meaning the Puritan clerics intended. Moreover, the attempt by the Puritan clerics to establish a fixed moral scheme for everyone is undone by the mobility of meaning of Hester's letter. It comes to mean "Able" then "Angel," a meaning completely at odds with what the clerics intended. Nature subverts moral government, Hawthorne argues in the novel, and the fate of this central symbol confirms that argument.

The narrative draws on the prevailing Puritan moral story, one in which redemption is attained through painful suffering for sins that some would consider simply the expression of natural passions, and it then ironically reworks those premises so that their values are reversed. Because Hawthorne endorses the view that sees nature as inherently moral and sexual passion as beyond moral schemes, the novel makes the Puritan moral story seem perverse and unnatural. Normally, the Puritan narrative of redemption would portray those who have sinned as evil and in need of moral supervision from holy men. But in this instance, the holy man is himself prone to natural passions. He fathers a child with a young woman. She, rather than being presented as a repository of negative or immoral traits, turns out to be one of the more moral characters in the novel. Her "progress" is not toward reconciliation with the conservative moral authorities; it is, rather, a progress away from the church toward a more natural, spontaneously generated morality that focuses on actually doing good for people instead of branding them as evil for having natural passions.

One important function in the conservative Puritan narrative would be the moment when the sinner accepts the judgment of the holy men and acknowledges his or her wrong. No such moment occurs in *The Scarlet Letter*. Instead, the two moments that might have fulfilled that narrative function – when Hester stands before the crowd on the scaffold in the market and the moment at the end when Dimmesdale mounts the scaffold with her and Pearl – serve a very different narrative goal and have a very different thematic purpose. Both are moments of defiance, when Hester proudly rejects the admonition of the Puritan elders and when Dimmesdale proudly adopts his natural family as his own. Rather than acknowledge guilt or confess to sin, he does what the virtuous Pearl asks of him and freely accepts his natural family as his own. Hawthorne thus creates an ironic version of the standard Puritan narrative of progress toward redemption and away from sin, assisted by the holy men and the holy teachings of the church. In his view, the church itself is evil, and progress consists of movement away from it and toward nature. *The Scarlet Letter* begins with the Puritan premise that sinners (those whose natural passions count as sins in the Puritan moral scheme, that is) should be punished. But Hawthorne immediately questions this premise by portraying his significant characters as rebels whose rebellion is justified. It too is an embodiment of the same natural spirituality that stands opposed to Puritan moral assumptions.

Form is essential to filmmaking because movies are in some respects nothing but exercises in technique. When you shoot a scene in a movie, you have to decide what form is appropriate to the ends you wish to achieve, be they thematic (getting an idea right) or representational (depicting a particular world accurately). You have to decide where to place the camera and what different effects different camera positions will create. You have to decide how to light the scene so as to suggest one emotional tone or another.

Will it be dark or light, and how will each one affect the audience's perceptions of the imagined reality? Similarly, in literature, one has to decide as a writer whether to be "light," to use a humorous tone even with serious material as James Joyce chooses to do in *Ulysses*, or to be "heavy," to describe things in such a way that even small things seem to bear universal significance as in the except from Hemingway. One must also place the writer's version of a camera – narrative voice – in a particular position by choosing which perspective to adopt on the events of the story – right behind the main character's ear or high up in the sky looking down on all the events and characters equally?

Citizen Kane is made with a great deal of technical virtuosity. If you pay attention to the way the filmmaker, Orson Welles, uses the camera when filming Charlie Kane, you'll find that he is often implying a criticism of Kane for his faults, which include grandiosity, egotism, and excess ambition. He shoots the film from different perspectives, so that Kane looks different depending on whose eyes we see him through. In one sequence, Kane gives a political campaign speech. The camera assumes the point of view or perspective of his young son who is watching. But then it switches to the perspective of someone watching from high up in the amphitheater.

Figure 1   *Citizen Kane*. Produced and directed by Orson Welles. 1941.

Figure 2   *Citizen Kane*. Produced and directed by Orson Welles. 1941.

Figure 3   *Citizen Kane*. Produced and directed by Orson Welles. 1941.

The perspective of his son makes Kane look huge, bigger than life, a real hero, a great man. But the perspective of the silent watcher makes him seem small. As the sequence unfolds, we learn that the watcher is a corrupt politician about whom Kane is talking in his speech. He says he intends to put the corrupt politician in jail. But the virtuous Kane is vulnerable. He is having an affair with a young woman, and the corrupt politician is about to blackmail him. What we see is ironic form at work: Kane thinks one thing, but we in the audience see another that contradicts what he thinks. He feels, mistakenly, that he has power, and the camera position reinforces that sense of things. But the ironic truth is that he is in someone else's power.

Consider the sequence that shows the celebration of the acquisition of the *Chronicle*. It contains several nice metaphors. It opens with a photograph that then becomes the real thing photographed – a group of men. The metaphor is that images have as much substance as reality for Charlie Kane. He is more concerned with how the newspaper looks than with what it actually is. Next, Kane is dancing with a line of women. The camera observes him from the perspective of his co-workers, Leland and Bernstein, who speak of him skeptically. The perspective suddenly shifts, and we see Leland and Bernstein and a window behind them. Notice that Kane now

Figure 4   *Citizen Kane*. Produced and directed by Orson Welles. 1941.

appears as a reflection on the glass of the window. Reflections have less substance than actual things, and here the theme of the clash between substance and image established at the beginning of the sequence continues. As the sequence evolves, smoke from a cigar drifts in front of the reflection. It too suggests a lack of substance, and it is associated with Charlie. Formalists notice that content or meaning is often determined by perspective or point of view, where you stand when you look at something or whose perspective you adopt in telling a story. In this sequence, you are put in the position of looking at Kane from the point of view of his good friend, Leland, who clearly is skeptical regarding Charlie. That skepticism is recorded in the images and metaphors that suggest a lack of substance.

Things to Look for in Literary and Cultural Texts

- What are the major elements of the work's form? Is the meaning of the work embedded as much in how it is done or written as in what it is about?

- How is the narrative organized or constructed? Can it be mapped as a logical structure of causes and consequences?

- What is the perspective from which the story is told and how does that affect what is told or can be told?

- What metaphors or images are used? What thematic purposes do the metaphors serve?

- How do such elements of poetic construction as rhyme and rhythm affect meaning?

2

Structuralism

Major Texts

Ferdinand de Saussure, *Course in General Linguistics*
Roman Jakobson and Morris Halle, *Fundamentals of Language*
Roland Barthes, *Mythologies*
Michel Foucault, *The Order of Things*

Major Ideas

- A structure is something that does not vary or change. It remains the same through time, and it is the same in different places. The skeleton of Homo sapiens is the same around the world; it has the same structure. It also remains the same over time. After humans achieve adulthood, they have the same skeletal structure until they die. A structure in human culture is something that is found everywhere and at all times. For example, oral folk-tales follow the same sequence of types of events (such as "the hero leaves home"), and myths from different cultures deal with the same universal issues in human life (such as how our civil or human side contends with our animal or natural side). In film stories, heroes with extraordinary abilities often solve problems such as rule-breaking or excess greed that threaten civil life. The same structure – "hero solves the problem of rule-breaking to ensure the survival of human civilization" – can be found in many different places. It is a universal structure of human culture.

An Introduction to Criticism: Literature / Film / Culture, First Edition. Michael Ryan.
© 2012 Michael Ryan. Published 2012 by Blackwell Publishing Ltd.

- Structuralism began in Linguistics. Structural Linguistics is concerned with the system of language that is distinct from spoken statements. The language system consists of all the rules of operation that allow spoken statements to be made by selecting and combining acoustic or written signs. Grammar is an important component of any language system; it defines how words can be meaningfully combined into statements. For Structural Linguists, language is both a structure and an event. When we speak, we engage in a speech event. We can only do so, however, if we have learned the system of our language and have it embedded in our brains. We may never engage in that exact same speech event again, but the structure of language in our brain must stay roughly the same if we are to continue communicating with our fellows. A structure stays the same and lasts through time, but an event happens just once. Language has structure because it is a system of rules and of sounds. Every time you speak, you draw on that grammar system and that dictionary of words. The rules of grammar allow sounds to have meaning and to function in communication with other practitioners of the language.

- Poems and movies are like language. They have structure and they are events. Each one is like a spoken sentence in a language. Each embodies a cultural language system and is made possible by the common understandings readers who participate in the same culture share. Cultural language systems are consistent and uniform within themselves; all the terms make sense in the same predictable way. But they can vary amongst themselves, with one literary system differing from another. For example, a hero in a movie like *The Searchers* might begin outside the law (a sign of his power) but end by accommodating himself to the law for the sake of the community he wishes to protect (a sign of the power of the law). In contrast, in a different literary textual system such as that of *The Scarlet Letter*, Reverend Dimmesdale breaks the law, and he seems bad initially, but then we learn that the law in question is really one that should be broken because it betrays the human heart. The sign for "law-breaker" becomes a sign for "virtue" by the end of the novel. To understand both the movie and the novel, you have to know the system of values and meanings that inform each work, the grammar that allows each image or word to be meaningful. That system is present in every image and every sentence; it is the structure hidden in the event.

- The differential principle is an important feature of structural analysis. According to it, no single part of a language has meaning in and of itself.

Its identity is made possible by its difference from and its connection to other parts of the language. In language, each word is determined by its difference from other words. "Hat" can have meaning as a sound only because it sounds different from "cat" or "mat." This is why many Structuralists say that identity is difference. Another name for difference is "relation" because difference really means that things exist in relation to one another. Movies and novels also are like language in that they consist of parts whose relations with each other generate meaning. The hero in the movie just described is different from the representative of religion and law in the movie, but he is also similar enough to him to ensure his accommodation with law by the end of the movie. In a similar way, the structure of a work of literature – the relations between parts – is what generates meaning in the literary work. Like the system of language, those relations are invisible, yet they make possible what we see on the page. Stories in literature are like acts of speech in language in that they embody a system that allows each term used (each character, each event in the narrative, each location, etc.) to have meaning. We know, for example, that Reverend Dimmesdale in *The Scarlet Letter* is in fact a good man because he is paired and contrasted with Roger Chillingworth, who is associated with the devil and with the betrayal of the sanctity of the human heart. In this example, contrast defines the identity of virtue.

- Linguistics used to study language as a set of names for things. But according to Structuralist Linguistics, language is an independent sign system in which the meaning of signs is determined by the language system itself and not by the linking of words and things. This is an important and a controversial idea because it draws attention to the fact that when we know the world, we do so through language, and the words of language connect as names to things in the world only because of agreements between language users that allow them to do so. The word for such agreements is "conventional." A convention is an agreement, and all words are conventional. "Tree" in English is "arbre" in French. There is no natural connection between the sounds or letters and the thing. The language system allows the sounds and letters to designate something in the world. All of our knowledge, inasmuch as it always occurs in language, is conventional or agreement-based. Structuralists took this idea fairly far, as we shall see in a moment.

- Words are signs that consist of two parts – a sound image or "signifier" and a mental image or a "signified." The word "tree" is a sound, and it means something in a language because it evokes a mental image of a particular object in the world. Language is a self-contained system that allows us to assign meaning to sounds that are then attached to mental images (such as "tree" or "book"), and we agree these sound-images will attach to things in the world. But the match-up between mental image and thing is entirely arbitrary. A tree could be called a cow in another language. What is important for Structuralism is how the different elements of the language system work through their relations to one another, not how the signs match up with things.

- Culture is like language in that it is a sign system that makes meaning for us. Everything from business to marriage is made possible by such cultural sign systems. Literature also is a self-contained system for generating meanings, and those meanings are only secondarily connected to the real world. Structuralists are more concerned with how the sign systems of literature, film, and culture operate than with how they refer to the world.

- Structuralism studies the enduring, universal aspect of the human experience as that manifests itself in literature and culture. But it is also concerned with how specific instances of sign systems function to manage our experience of the world. The nightly news is such a sign system, as is an advertisement for perfume.

Major Terms

Language System, Speech   All language has two components – spoken speech and the language system that permits speech to occur. The system consists of all the rules of operation that are at work when one speaks and makes coherent statements within the language.

Sign/Signifier/Signified   Words are signs, and each word has two parts – a signifier, or a sound image such as "rat" or "hat" and a signified, or the mental image with which the sound is associated. When we hear "rat," it evokes an idea or image of a rat in our minds; we do not need an actual rat present to understand the word. Semiology (or Semiotics) is the study of sign systems.

Arbitrary/Arbitrariness   The relation between a word and a thing is entirely arbitrary. There is no necessary link.

Difference   The identity of each word or linguistic sign is formed by its difference from other words within the language system. "Hat" is a meaningless sound unless it is juxtaposed to "fat." "Hat" has an identity both as a sound and as a meaning by virtue of its slight difference from similar sounds. In the language system, there are no identities – things that stand entirely on their own. There are only differences. Nothing in language has an identity outside its relations to other terms within the system.

Code   A sign has meaning by reference to a code, a set of connected terms that provide the sign with meaning and allow it to function in communication. More broadly in literature and culture, code is used to characterize aspects of form (the color code used in a movie that assigns meaning to particular colors, for example) as well as aspects of meaning (the behavioral code that assigns meaning to certain actions).

Syntagm   A sentence in any language has two dimensions. It flows through time and consists of elements that are linked in a chain of sounds or written signs. The term for this first dimension is "syntagm." This dimension is also diachronic, which means it moves across time.

Paradigm   The other dimension of all sentences is spatial or static, and it is called "paradigm." A paradigm consists of all the available options for any one moment in a sentence in a language. A paradigm set for the noun place in a sentence would consist of all the possible fillers for that slot. This dimension of the sentence is synchronic because all the possible filers for any one slot exist simultaneously.

Metaphor/Metonymy   Metaphors link things through similarity and substitution (*sun* resembles *love*) while metonymy links things through actual connections (*sail* for *boat*). Metaphor is the axis of language (substitution) most associated with poetry, while metonymy is the axis of language (contiguity) most associated with fictional prose.

Summary and Discussion

Structuralist Linguistics is distinguished by its focus on language understood as a system of rules and conventions that make everyday speech communication possible. The system is implied in every speech act. It is the embedded program that allows us to use language. Rather than focus on language understood as a collection of statements, Structuralism focuses on language considered as a self-enclosed system whose rules and conventions allow statements to be made.

Language allows us to manipulate the world by proclaiming laws, preaching gospels, giving instructions, teaching information, dictating letters, typing in commands, and the like. But language works because it has internal rules that allow certain sounds to match up with certain ideas or mental images that in turn signify or mean certain things or actions or operations in the non-linguistic world. For Structuralists, those match-ups of sounds and things, words and ideas, are less important than the rules and conventions that make them possible. Imagine a choice between studying the figures and actions of a computer game like World of Warcraft or studying the computer program and the code that makes it possible. Structuralists choose the latter, and they see the game's figures and actions primarily in terms of the way they embody the code.

Words help us to manipulate the world around us, but language is able to do this because it is a world unto itself. It is like an independent machine whose operations are due entirely to its own rules, and the fact that it allows us to do things to the world is secondary. The chain on a chainsaw works because it is part of a larger mechanism, not because it makes a particular kind of cut in a tree. Yet in language we often assume that words are determined by what they do. They are names for things. We ignore the fact that words are sounds and mental images in a complex machine or system called language. Like the chain on a chainsaw that works because of the machine attached to it, words work because of the machinery of the language system that is attached to every one of them. Structuralist Linguistics is concerned with this dual nature of language. Language is impersonal and shared (like the rules of chess), but it is also a field of infinite variation linked to the actual use of the language.

The consequences of Structuralism for literary and cultural criticism have been profound. Thinkers have been especially attracted by the Structuralist idea that language is a self-enclosed semiotic system. They linked that idea to cultural institutions and practices such as advertising and journalism. We know the world through signs, and signs can be used to manipulate how we know the world. The Structuralists also were concerned with how discourse (see Chapter 1 above) plays a role in knowledge. A discourse provides tools for knowing the world by allowing things to be named in a certain way that makes sense. A discourse also, however, establishes rules for what counts as good knowledge, and it excludes other kinds of knowledge. For many decades in the US literary academy, for example, the New Critics were dominant, and their discourse was one that favored complex symbolic poetry over other kinds of literature. Their discourse excluded or diminished the importance of writing by women and non-Whites because such writing did not match the New Critical norm or standard. It was often historical, sociological, sentimental, and political. It was not about universal truths. That dominant discourse has since been challenged and changed. Now the literary academy is much more open to a variety of different kinds of writing, and there is no one dominant literary-critical discourse.

Roland Barthes, perhaps the leading Structuralist critic of his era, used these ideas to generate a way of criticizing both literature and culture. In his book *Mythologies* he examined everything from detergent advertisements to travel guide books for how they use signs to substitute "myths" for an accurate representation of reality. Jean Baudrillard, a sociologist, argued that we live in a consumer society in which codes take the place of reality; differences among cars, for example, create meaning for us that is more important than the meaning we might attain in our lives by actually accomplishing something great.

Codes and the way they determine the meaning of things are a central concern of Structuralist literary critics. A code resembles a dictionary; it supplies the meaning of a word, a sign, an event, or a thing. In the sartorial code of the European military in the 19th century, only certain kinds of soldiers were allowed to wear certain colors such as red or "Prussian blue." The colors, in the code, signified honor, prestige, and status. For others not supposedly in possession of those qualities to wear them would have besmirched the character of those who did. Not all codes are so prescriptive. Sometimes writers and filmmakers choose to set action in particular places that within a cultural code have certain meanings. The post-World War II film *Mildred Pierce* begins in an upscale beach house, but then the action shifts to what in the 1940s would have been called a "dive," a bar where cheap liquor is consumed in smoke-filled rooms. The choice of settings was significant within the cultural codes of the era.

Examples of Structuralist Analysis

Criticism conducted under Structuralist auspices notices how literary or cultural language systems generate particular realities. The choice of words or images is crucial for determining what kind of experienced reality the reader or viewer will encounter. Literary and cultural language systems are projective in that they do not so much describe or represent an existing reality as generate an effect of reality. They create an imagined world that is laden with value. In the American South, Blacks were more easily lynchable because of the words used to characterize them in White discourse. Consider these two examples. Richard Wright, in *Uncle Tom's Children*, describes the actions of a lynch mob:

> 'Jack! Jack! Don leve me! Ah wanna see im!'
> 'They're bringin im over the hill, sweetheart!'
> 'AH WANNA BE THE FIRST PUT A ROPE ON THA BLACK BASTARDS
>   NECK!'
> 'Let's start the fire!'
> 'Heat the tar!'
> 'Ah got some chains t chain im.'
> Bring im over this way!'
> 'Chris, Ah wished Ah hada drink …'
> Big Boy saw men moving over the hill. Among them was a long dark spot.
> Ta mu be Bobo; tha mus be Bob theys carryin …
> They had started the song again:
> 'We'll hang ever nigger t a sour apple tree …'
> There were women singing now. Their voices made the song round and full.

The brutality of the language licenses a similar brutality of action. Compare that use of language to the language used by William Faulkner, a racist Southern writer, in *Light in August*, who describes similar events from the other, White, side of the racial divide. In this passage, Joe August, a man who is of mixed race and who has murdered a White woman, is described just before he is killed and castrated by a White man. Faulkner, like many Southerners, believed that the races should not mix, and that to do so was like breeding cats with dogs. Notice how Black blood is characterized negatively while White blood is characterized positively:

> But his blood would not be quiet, let him save it. It would not be either one
> or the other and let his body save itself. Because the black blood drove him
> first to the negro cabin. And then the white blood drove him out of there, as
> it was the black blood that snatched up the pistol and the white blood which
> would not let him fire it. And it was the white blood which sent him to the
> minister. … It was the black blood which swept him by his own desire
> beyond the aid of any man, swept him up into that ecstasy out of a black
> jungle … And then the black blood failed him again, as it must have in crises
> all his life. He did not kill the minister. He merely struck him with the pistol
> and ran on and crouched behind that table and defied the black blood for the

last time, as he had been defying it for thirty years. He crouched behind that overturned table and let them shoot him to death, with that loaded and unfired pistol in his hand.

White blood represents all that is good. It is associated with civilized restraint and religion, while Black blood is associated with a tendency toward violence, a loss of restraint, and the "jungle," a place outside civilization. In this way, the lynching of the Black man is justified as somehow his own fault. Faulkner's language for characterizing Blacks in the novel draws on codes common in the American South to justify lynching. Blacks are "naturally" or by "blood" dangerous and violent.

Similarly, films made within certain strong ideological or political codes of representation often use strong imagery to depict characters that, within that particular political ideology, are considered dangerous. In *Falling Down*, for example, Latino working-class youths are depicted as irrational, vicious threats to sane, rational, hard-working Whites. The codes of conservative White culture in the US inform the way the film chooses images to represent "ethnic" characters. The choice of images allocates value differently, so that a negative inflection falls on the Latinos and a positive one is given to the White character. In one scene, he stands still while he is circled by a group of Latino youths. The contrasts suggests that he represents stability (even stability of values) while they are like predators, hoping to take what is not theirs. The image embodies White conservatives' fears of immigrants and what they seek in America.

In the culture of public discourse (journalism, political speech, rumor, etc.), words are important for mobilizing belief and affect so that the interests of a political group such as a nation, or an economic group such as a social class, are served. The "War on Terror," for example was invented by political conservatives in the US. Words like "terrorism" came to name Islamic opponents of US interests, and the repetition of the word in the media and in public discussion successfully transformed Islamic opposition into something entirely negative. A typological word like "terrorism" came to sum up a very diverse field of positions with multiple causes. One effect was that the US's role in instigating violent opposition to its interests by its continuing support for the colonization of Palestine by Israel and by its stationing of armies in the Islamic holy land became invisible. Another effect of the term is to codify all Arabic opposition as terrorist, even if it is a legitimate response to an illegal invasion, as was the case in Iraq. (The US invaded without UN approval.)

Words also serve the role of securing group identity by designating members of other groups negatively. For example, in the culture wars in America after World War II, marijuana was stigmatized and removed from medicine. The term "marijuana" itself began to be used because it was a Mexican term for low-grade tobacco. Black jazz lovers and musicians were associated by the dominant White culture with marijuana and, by implication, with moral depravity. Interestingly, at the same time "drink" became a term for hard liquor, which was often abused on a routine basis by Whites (the famous two-martini lunch in business culture). But drink was considered moral, and was even taken on Sunday mornings if Sloane Wilson, the author of *The Man in the Gray Flannel Suit*, is to be believed. Yet drink, as Mothers Against Drunk Driving eventually pointed out, was often fatal. Marijuana, on the other hand, had proven positive medical uses. An irrational choice by one social group was imposed on society by the use of derogatory words for stigmatized drugs and those, like Black jazz musicians, who used them. Things began to change when young poets like Allan Ginsberg came along and forged new, more positive, terms such as "angel headed hipster" for them.

Structuralist criticism is also concerned with how literature constructs a system of meaning based on the relations between terms or parts of the system. Each work is a language system of its own. It processes signifying elements – signs – and turns them into a system of interrelated terms whose meaning or significance arises from their interrelations within the system. Such order tends to be both spatial and temporal. Spatial order often is moral: a good character is juxtaposed to a bad character; or a world of one kind that is positively valued is posed against a different kind of social or cultural world that bears a negative value. Temporal order is constructed through narration usually by creating logical sequences of events such that an event with one value leads to a consequence that has another value. A decision to betray trust might be followed by a description of events in which the betrayal leads to loss. In one editing sequence in *Mildred Pierce*, Mildred, recently divorced, makes love with a playboy, and in the next image her husband learns that their daughter is dying. The editing evolution is moral, and Mildred is blamed for doing something that in the moral code of the era (the 1940s) would have been coded as immoral or inappropriate.

Consider the relations between parts of *The Scarlet Letter*. The narrative evolves from an initial defiance of the law on the part of Hester Prynne, who has had an illegitimate child and is forced to wear a scarlet letter A on her chest (for "Adultery") by the Puritan community in which she lives, to an apparent acceptance of the law on the part of her lover, Arthur Dimmesdale, a minister whose guilt is kept hidden until the end, when he chooses to reveal his part in Hester's shame while standing before the community on the scaffold where criminals are usually punished. The meaning of the novel hinges on how we interpret that narrative trajectory. It also hinges on two other characters – Pearl, the illegitimate child of Arthur and Hester, and Chillingworth, Hester's legitimate husband whom she does not love. Pearl is the embodiment of natural freedom and of a nature whose spontaneous processes are portrayed by Hawthorne as virtuous in and of themselves, apart entirely from moral value schemes such as the one that allows the Puritans to brand Hester a sinner. Chillingworth represents the worst aspect of those moral value schemes. A cold, heartless man with no sense of empathy for others, he would "dissect" Pearl rather than celebrate her naturally free spirit. Pearl urges Dimmesdale to reveal the truth, and when he does, therefore, it should be interpreted as a gesture that affirms the values she represents. Rather than being a compromise with the authority of Puritan moral government, his revelation of his "sin" and his death on the public scaffold at the end is a freely chosen act of atonement for having done wrong to his natural family, not to the conservative churchmen. It displays his true, natural, passionate self – a self the Puritan authorities would brand as "sinful" but that Hawthorne, by associating it in the structure of the novel with Pearl, wants us to see in a different light, as something more positive and affirmative. The structure of relations between parts in a literary text can therefore assist in interpreting it properly.

A Structuralist critic would also note that the novel is about signs and about the arbitrary character of our cultural signs. Some try to make the signs that are dominant in any one society seem natural and absolute. They try to make meaning seem to arise from the nature of things and not from some arbitrary and debatable convention imposed on people by those with the power to do so. In Puritan New England, the ones with the power to impose absolute meanings were the church authorities (who also were the political authorities). And the sign/meaning they seek to impose in the novel is "sinner." Hester Prynne is branded with an A because the authorities decide she has that meaning and that the sign for sinner should be attached to her to indicate that that is her identity and her meaning. But, from the outset, Hester shrugs off this semiotic imposition. She turns the sign to her own uses and makes it into a sign of creativity, of beauty, of virtue, and of an innate natural spirituality. Throughout the novel, Hawthorne educates the reader to think that those branded as "sinners" are in fact good people who are being mistreated by the authorities. The Puritan moral code is, in his eyes, perverse. It makes those that nature and, for Hawthorne, divinity in nature have endowed with virtue seem to be just the opposite of what they truly are.

The narrative of the novel can thus be said to carry out an inversion of the initial premise with which it began. That premise was both semiotic and moral, and it consisted of a binary opposition between virtue and vice; Hester was given a sign that was supposed to mean "Adulterer," but during the course of the narrative, that initial premise is inverted and Hester comes to represent moral virtue rather than moral vice. The novel engages in what might be called a recoding of the dominant meaning system of the time, the codification of human action that the Puritans of the 17th century tried to impose on society. It does so by switching the value of one action so that its meaning changes radically: adultery becomes virtue. In consequence, the moral scheme or code that

Figure 5   *Citizen Kane*. Produced and directed by Orson Welles. 1941.

branded it as moral vice is thrown into question. Narratology is the study of such grammatical transformations in narratives.

The character of Charles Foster Kane in *Citizen Kane* is based on a real person (William Randolph Hearst), but in his fictional characterization codes of representation are at work that are cultural and cinematic. An obvious place to start would be Kane's drive to accumulate too many things. The opening newsreel segment draws attention to this great number of things and their enormous magnitude. The newsreel uses representational codes appropriate to a "great man." Kane is depicted as worthy of attention, a man whose words are important and whose pronouncements about the world are worth listening to. In today's parlance, he is worthy of being pursued by paparazzi who shoot images of him through fences. There is a feeling of grandeur about him that is matched by his large possessions. Having cited the code of the great man at the outset, the film then sets about challenging it. By the end, Kane is alone in a huge mansion, abandoned by the woman he loved because of his egotism. He can collect people and things, huge numbers of them, but he cannot get what he really wants in life – a warm and affectionate emotional attachment. The code changes. Huge numbers by the end of the film suggest not greatness and grandeur but emptiness and misery.

Things to Look for in Literary and Cultural Texts

- What is the structure of the work? Can you draw a map of it such that all of its elements make sense in relation to one another? Can the structure be seen as embodying a scheme of values? Are the characters the bearers of values? What might they be said to represent?

- Does the narrative follow a logical progression? Does it embody an argument regarding the world – i.e., is it making a statement regarding values or people in the world, and if so, how does the narrative work out that argument through opposition and resolution?

- Is the meaning of the work shaped and determined by codes and signs? What are those codes and how do they manifest themselves in signs within the work?

3

Historical Criticism

Major Texts

E. P. Thompson, *The Making of the English Working Class*
Raymond Williams, *Culture and Society*
Ian Watt, *The Rise of the Novel*
Vernon Parrington, *Main Currents in American Thought*
Stephen Greenblatt, *Shakespearean Negotiations*

Major Ideas

- Historical information can explain a cultural text by providing meaning for events and characters that is not locatable within the text itself.

- What we think of as "history" itself changes with time. The history of England once was concerned with issues of royal succession and court politics. A new generation of historians told the history of England from the perspective of common people whose everyday concerns struck these historians as being as important as the power machinations of England's ruling families and political elite. Other historians focus on women and workers. What counts as important in history depends on which historical characters' lives are selected for telling.

- Historians used to be concerned with politics and economics. They have come to recognize the importance of culture in the evolution of society. Traditional economic, political, and social history has now been

An Introduction to Criticism: Literature / Film / Culture, First Edition. Michael Ryan.
© 2012 Michael Ryan. Published 2012 by Blackwell Publishing Ltd.

supplemented by cultural history. Religion, for example, is a cultural force that is now recognized to be of great importance in the development of a country like the United States.

- Historical change makes for changes in culture. In England, as society changed from the late 18th century to the 19th, novels about the landed aristocracy and genteel life gave way to more realist novels about working people, such as George Eliot's *Adam Bede*. With the expansion of the right to vote, the voices of such people became more important in English society and English novel-writing.

- Historians differ over what is the major influence or force at any one moment in history, and they differ over how change comes about. Some contend that economics is most important. For economic historians, the making and consuming of things is the most important feature of a society. Social historians are more concerned with how people lived in the past, what they did every day, how they practiced their beliefs or went about their business, how they interacted with one another and formed different kinds of communities and organizations, and the like. For political historians, a society is defined and determined by who runs it. The distribution of power is as important as the distribution of food. Political parties are the expression of both economics and social life, and the major changes that occur in the world are the result of political action.

- Each moment of history is characterized not only by events and institutions but also by discourses in contention with each other. The European monarchies that were almost destroyed by the French Revolution were sustained by discourses (ways of talking, writing, and discussing) that justified the rule of kings and queens. A new democratic discourse emerged in the 18th century, in the writings of such people as Jean-Jacques Rousseau, to challenge the discourse of monarchical authority. The French Revolution was as much a struggle between discourses (and the ideas embedded in them) as it was a struggle between social groups.

Major Terms

Renaissance   A cultural movement in western Europe from the 14th to the 16th centuries that witnessed a rebirth of cultural and intellectual creativity.

Early Modern Period   The period after the late Middle Ages, from 1500 to 1800, when nation-states formed in Europe and colonies were created in North America.

Puritanism   A movement within English Protestantism in the 16th and 17th centuries that sought to purify the Church of England. In America, the Puritans were associated with the belief that some, who were considered "holy," were superior to others. But Puritan doctrine also emphasized freedom of conscience and is often said to have laid the ideological basis for the American Revolution against the British empire.

Restoration   After the English Civil War, the monarchy was restored (1661), and during the period after that event, theaters, which had been banished under the Puritans, flourished; Restoration drama is known for its bawdiness.

Romanticism   Literary history is defined in part by movements such as Romanticism, which occurred in Europe in the late 18th and early 19th centuries. Romantics favored emotion over reason and advocated a spiritualist concept of nature.

Aestheticism   If Romanticism reacted to the Rationalism of the 18th century, Aestheticism responded to the Positivism (the privileging of analysis and factual knowledge over imagination and feeling) of the mid-19th century. In the 1880s especially, Aesthetes such as Walter Pater argued that one should relish one's immediate experience, especially the experience of art.

Empire/Imperialism   The Age of Empire lasted from 1875 to 1914, as many European countries seized parts of the globe for economic reasons (markets and raw materials), but England was an active imperial power for many centuries before that. The issue of empire became a matter of public debate in the late 19th century. Only in the 20th century, however, in the wake of two world wars, would Britain withdraw from colonies such as Palestine, Kenya, and India. The US engaged in imperial activity at this time as well, fueled by a group of domestic conservatives who felt America stood to lose economically if it did not imitate the European imperial countries.

Modernism   A major cultural movement of the early 20th century was Modernism, which rejected the ideal of realism, developed styles based on the new industrial technologies, and sought to create a new world through aesthetic radicalism. Many Modernists deliberately eschewed representation altogether and sought to create new art forms (paintings such as Kandinsky's *The Great Gate of Kiev* or Joyce's novel *Finnegans Wake*) that spoke entirely new, non-representational languages.

Great Depression/New Deal   Wars are often crucial in cultural history, but so are major economic cataclysms such as the Great Depression of the 1930s, which gave rise to conservative movements such as Fascism and Nazism that brought about World War II. The economic collapse also fostered leftwing cultural movements such as Expressionism in Europe and social realism in the US. Expressionism became an influential cinematic style as film noir in the US. The New Deal, the liberal response to the Depression that used government as a tool of economic recovery, initiated a long debate over the role of government in economic life that continues to the present in the US between conservatives (anti-government) and liberals (pro-government).

Post-Modernism   According to Marxist cultural historians, Modernism has ended and been superseded by a new era called Post-Modernism, characterized by the emergence of a global economy, the power of finance capital, and the abandonment of the old Fordist model of industry, whereby workers were paid good wages so that they could buy consumer goods, and worked in factories producing goods for their own nations. Globalization means that goods made in China now supply the needs of North America, and North American factory workers are increasingly replaced by much lower-paid Chinese workers. The goal of modern capitalism has shifted toward a high return on investment premised on wages being kept as low as possible.

Globalization   The contemporary era is defined by an expansion of free market capitalism around the globe. This movement, led by governments such as that of China and North American corporations such as Wal-Mart, is opposed by anarchists and anti-capitalism activists, who see it as fostering economic inequality.

Summary and Discussion

History is a record of past events, but it is also the past frozen and held still for study. It is as if one walked into a room that a moment before had been busy with life and that had been emptied suddenly by some silent command.

There would be traces of the people everywhere – half-filled mugs, pens put down, letters half-finished, work half-done – but no one would be there. And none could return. No further amendments could be made in the draft report, no more finishing touches added to a letter. The record would be what it was at that moment, and it would be all you would have to use in figuring out who the people were, how they thought, what they felt, and why they acted as they did. That is what is called the archive, history that consists of objects left over – written texts or visual documents, buildings and clothes, works of art and institutions such as particular kinds of law courts or customary practices. History is what humanity sees when it looks over its shoulder, but it is also what we see when we look around in the present, because we are producing history all the time. Each moment that passes is a moment that has just become historical.

I usually teach American literature and culture historically. I ask students to read online history texts, and I provide them with a historical time-line within which to understand what they are reading or viewing. I find that meaning is historical in some way or another for pretty much all cultural texts. Some meanings are internal to a text and have to do with structure and form. But at some point even a good formal analysis reaches a point where history has to take over. It adds something that Formalist analysis cannot explain. What it adds is a larger field of meaning in which a text can and should be situated in order to be understood fully. Such fields of meaning can extend back into the past, or they can extend around a text in a way that connects it with adjacent parts of reality.

For example, when I teach Hawthorne's *The Scarlet Letter*, I have students do readings about the Whig and Democratic parties in the 1840s, when Hawthorne, a fervent Democrat, lived and wrote. The novel, it turns out, is in fact a highly polemical text that engages a current debate about the proper relation between church and state. In 1849, when the novel was written, Jacksonian Democracy had just changed America, taking power away from the wealthy elite which had used government to foster economic development favorable to its own financial interests. The Federalists and the Whigs used government money to build an infrastructure of canals and roads suitable to the kind of economic development their constituents in the business community favored. Such industrial development encouraged the conversion of independent yeoman farmers into wage laborers and deprived them, according to Jacksonian ideology, of their manly independence. Such policies were even considered to be an affront to the spirit of God in nature, since artificial contrivances such as banks, tariffs, and government-chartered monopolies were unnatural and did not allow the natural economy to take is own course. They interfered with the spontaneous actions of nature that were expressions of God's will and presence. Both Jacksonians and Whigs thought about politics in religious terms. The Whigs used government to promote moral behavior (through such things as anti-adultery laws), while to the Democrats, such "church and state" Yankeeism constituted interference with divinity in nature. If the Whigs sought to create a more self-disciplined labor force suitable for a modern industrial economy, the Jacksonian Democrats considered the voice of the people to be the voice of God, and they contended that government should be limited so as to foster the free development of people's natural talents.

The Whig ideal of moral government comes across in the novel as being harmful to naturally good people and as an affront to divinity in nature. The Democrats favored the theology of natural revelation because it licensed their belief that government should not place artificial moral restrictions on people through legislation. Nature should be left alone. And that indeed is the argument of the novel. The most natural character, Pearl, is also the most naturally virtuous. She represents the truth that the contrived, repressive, and punitive morality of the Whigs (and Puritans) betrays and harms. When, at the end of the novel, Dimmesdale stands up to the Puritan authorities, one senses that Hawthorne meant as well to portray a rebellion against Whig authorities that would regulate and monitor all aspects of life.

A different way of characterizing this historical reading would be to say that *The Scarlet Letter* marks a line of contact between discourses in contention with one another. New Historicism was concerned with the way literary texts fit into larger discourses whose purpose was to solidify a particular social reality by fostering belief. A sympathetic reader of *The Scarlet Letter*, for example, would come away feeling more skeptical of the Whig discourse that argued that a holy moral elite that has risen above all natural passion deserves to exercise moral government over others, especially over working-class immigrant people who do not even share, always, the Whigs' Protestant beliefs.

Examples of Historical Analysis

"Polemic" comes from the Greek word *polemos*, which means battle or war. Given the divisions within humanity, many of our cultural products are statements against something else; they are battles with an adversary.

In Sophocles' play *The Eumenides*, the goddess Athena convinces the Furies to give up a vindictive model of justice in favor of one based on forgiveness. It is a polemical play that advocates one value scheme and rejects another. It was written in Greece in the fifth century BC, and it reflects a change in Greek culture away from tribal warfare and toward city-state life, away from wars of revenge and toward greater civility that would allow very different people to inhabit the same space without violence. Not all cultural works are as polemical, but all generally make a point, and most points are made against other points. We define good by saying it is not evil, and we usually have something quite specific in mind for each quality or category.

One of my favorite cultural polemics comes from a quite polemical time in US cultural history – the 1930s, the era of the Great Depression and the New Deal, a liberal government program designed to ease economic distress through state action. Conservatives hated it because it took some of their wealth in the form of higher taxes and used it for the common good. It also made for a more even playing field between rich and poor, which placed wealthy conservatives at a disadvantage since their wealth depended on maintaining an uneven economic playing field. Liberals supported it because it enabled their ideal of building a more fair and just society. In 1933, Warner Brothers made *The Gold Diggers of 1933*, a movie about "showgirls" in theaters in New York city who played parts in musicals. It's a comedy, but it makes a serious point. In one sequence, soldiers from World War I are shown parading; then the image switches to a Depression-era breadline, and one sees the same soldiers begging for food because there is no work for them. Immediately afterwards, one of the showgirls sings a song about how one should help others. In terms of rhetoric, this is a "plea," an appeal for assistance. And the movie itself argues that point. Wealthy people are depicted as initially skeptical regarding the motives of the impoverished showgirls, who they take to be "gold-diggers," girls out to lure wealthy men with sex in order to get their money. But the girls turn the tables on the wealthy men and prove that they are indeed hard-working and virtuous; they don't want their money. When they realize this, the wealthy men convert to a kinder and more generous attitude toward the poor. They see that they deserve help and are not irresponsible and lazy. The film advocates a change of attitude on the part of the wealthy that would at the time have been beneficial to the New Deal.

Like so many cultural works, *Gold Diggers* is a rhetorical statement within a polemical cultural field. What it is as a text is only half the matter. It is in fact doing battle with any number of other statements within the discursive field in which it is located, statements on the part of conservatives and the wealthy against the liberal effort to assist the poor through government programs, programs that would tax the rich. Understandably, wealthy conservatives resisted, and their rhetorical efforts are a taken-for-granted background of the movie. It speaks against them, and their statements appear in the film in the form of the wealthy characters whose doubts would have to be turned around for the rhetorical effort of the film (and of the New Deal itself) to succeed.

A few years later, in 1936, those wealthy conservatives found a voice of their own in a film advocating their position. *My Man Godfrey* concerns a wealthy man who in a fit of despair over a lost love decides to go live with the "bums" on "skid row." Picked up as a lark by a wealthy family, he becomes their butler, and he sets about reforming their world using sound conservative principles. They are profligate and wasteful rather than industrious and self-restrained. The women are "out of control" and they waste the hard-working father's wealth. The mother has a lover, Carlo, who is an intellectual and an artist. He is depicted as a "free-loader," someone who does nothing and eats a lot. The girls of the family lack a moral compass: they party all night and break the law for random fun. Godfrey restores order to the family universe. With his guidance, the father once again "takes control," throws Carlo out, and reasserts his authority over his wife. At the same time, Godfrey, relying on an innate talent for such things, salvages the family finances through a timely investment.

In this film a heroic conservative individualist armed with innate virtues such as industry, moral restraint, and fortitude triumphs without government assistance. He rises from poverty back to wealth because he uses his own entrepreneurial initiative (and a chance donation of pearls worth a great deal of money). That is the conservative ideal, and at the time it was held up as a model that answered the liberal call for government assistance for the poor through taxation of the rich. Taxes should not be raised on the wealthy, this film argues. The wealthy should instead themselves use the money to foster enterprises that create jobs.

Because liberalism asks us to put the community before self-interest, *My Man Godfrey* depicts communities negatively. The family community is associated with madness, animality, and immorality. Without a strong, firm moral leader, the film argues, society falls apart and loses a proper sense of direction. Women depart from their appropriate roles, and "foreigners" and intellectuals guide society in wrong directions. This polemic is in striking contrast to the depiction of community in *Gold Diggers*. That film is famous for song and dance sequences designed by Busby Berkeley that emphasized synchronized action by a large group. The film's camerawork also emphasizes connections between people of different classes and races. In an advertisement for the liberal ideal of an inclusive diverse society, the camera moves laterally or horizontally to establish relations within the same visual space between different characters who represent different social constituencies. It is a film that promotes a quite positive vision of community.

At the time, wealthy conservatives were associated with an attitude of exclusion toward those who were not "native-born" or Anglo-Saxon Protestant Americans. That attitude is evident in the harsh way *Godfrey* treats the character of Carlo, who is reminiscent of the Jews and the bohemian intellectuals who were detested by conservatives at the time. The camerawork in *Godfrey* uses "cut away" editing to emphasize the separateness of the superior, self-controlled male individualists from the female-dominated community, which is portrayed as mildly hysterical. In one sequence, Carlo acts like an ape to entertain one of the daughters, and the hysteria of the community is juxtaposed through editing with Godfrey's calmly observant, detached image of dutiful and responsible labor. He is the model of the industrious conservative individualist who must bring "order" to the out-of-control community. Conservatives at the time were enthralled by the idea of leaders who imposed order from above on society. World War II would dispel that fascination with the likes of Adolf Hitler, who was conservative magazine *Time*'s "man of the year" in 1939.

If we saw these films today, we might mistake them for harmless entertainment, and indeed they are that to a degree. But if you place them in history, they acquire additional meaning as polemical statements against one another. *Gold Diggers* was made just when the worst of the Depression was making itself felt. Unemployment reached 50 percent in some parts of the country in the early 1930s. Many men walked the streets; some women prostituted themselves. No social welfare programs existed to assist them. The government, under conservative auspices, had for years adopted a hands-off attitude toward the economy and the world of business. With businessmen in charge of government throughout the 1920s, the wealthy became much wealthier, inequality grew, and a profligate lifestyle developed amongst the social elite. That came to a crashing halt in 1929, and the economy grew worse for several years. Franklin Roosevelt was elected in 1931, and in 1932 began to create new government programs to create jobs and to foster economic recovery. *Gold Diggers* speaks to that moment of hope, of joint effort, and of helpfulness toward others. By the mid-1930s, however, conservatives had begun to bridle at the new powers of the federal government. They especially resented new higher tax rates that funded the new expanded role for the state in the economy. Radical movements began to emerge on the left and right of the liberal Democrats in charge of the New Deal. Those new movements called for the redistribution of wealth or for populist alternatives to the New Deal. The election of 1935 was marked by bitter rhetoric and by Roosevelt's famous attack on "economic royalists." *Godfrey* is a rejoinder by those very royalists, and one senses what Roosevelt meant in the opening sequence, when Godfrey is called "Duke" by one of his fellow "bums." He is, in other words – appearances to the contrary – a natural nobleman or aristocrat, a superior individual who will save society through superior natural talents. Conservatives believed that some were better than others, and that was why they were wealthy. But they had to do more than sit on their wealth and engage in luxury consumption, the film argues; they had to invest and spur the creation of jobs if they were to answer the challenge the New Deal posed to their power. That was the position they had come to by 1936, when the film appeared.

So with a little history to help one, films like these display their meanings more fully.

Citizen Kane belongs to the same era and to the same debates as *Gold Diggers* and *Godfrey*. The newspaper magnate William Randolph Hearst,

Figure 6 *Citizen Kane*. Produced and directed by Orson Welles. 1941.

the figure on whom Kane is based, was a leading liberal in the early 20th century. He supported and funded the candidacy of Democrat William Jennings Bryan for president. But Hearst by the 1930s had become much more conservative. Progressives felt he had betrayed their cause of social reform and greater economic equality. The film suggests that his progressive ideals were not what they appeared to be from the outset. If you study the "statement of principles" sequence, you will notice that Welles uses lighting to suggest that Kane is self-deluded. He first stands at the window looking out on the city. He then says he is going to redo the front page of the newspaper again, even though it will mean extra expense and extra work for the laborers who do the printing. But that does not matter to Kane. He is more concerned with his ideas and his will. He writes the principles on a piece of paper, and as he walks forward to the table from the window his face enters darkness. Leland, the skeptical friend, points out that Kane has used the word "I" at the start of each statement of principle. That and the darkness of the image suggest that Kane is not seeing himself clearly; he imagines he is a man of the people, but in truth, he is a megalomaniac.

Things to Look for in Literary and Cultural Texts

- How is the historical moment present in the work? How is the work – in language, form, and theme – a product of its particular historical era?

- Do some research on the time period when the work was written. What was going on that might have been a significant influence on the work?

- Does the work make an argument that is part of a contemporary debate?

- How are the characters in the work "historical"? How do they represent types or figures who are specific to a particular time?

- Are the positions the author takes or the values and ideals the work endorses shaped by historical circumstances?

- Finally, does the work pertain to a particular discourse and does it contend with another discourse?

4

Psychoanalysis and Psychology

Major Texts

Sigmund Freud, *The Interpretation of Dreams*
Melanie Klein, *The Psychoanalysis of Children*
John Bowlby, *Attachment*
Donald Winnicott, *Playing and Reality*
Jacques Lacan, *Écrits*

Major Ideas

- The life of the mind is a mixture of cognition and emotion, conscious awareness and unconscious process, rational self-directed behavior and instinct-driven action. It is difficult therefore to take writers or artists "at their word." One must also look behind what is said in a text and analyze what the psychic sources might be of the fantasies and emotions one encounters there. Texts are often themselves "symptoms," indicators of illness or of a troubled personal history. But writers are also astute observers, and sometimes they describe psychological aspects of human life with great insight. They depict for us troubled emotions or upset relationships that resonate with our own lives or that allow access to general aspects of human emotional and psychic life.

- Psychoanalysis pictures the mind as part conscious and part unconscious. We all have an unconscious, a realm from which feelings well up

An Introduction to Criticism: Literature / Film / Culture, First Edition. Michael Ryan.
© 2012 Michael Ryan. Published 2012 by Blackwell Publishing Ltd.

or thoughts emerge unexpectedly. It is part of "us" but we do not control its operations. Psychoanalysts believe it is where banished feelings, desires, and thoughts go that our conscious mind or ego cannot accept for one reason or another (personal history, social pressures, cultural norms, etc.). Some feelings and thoughts are repressed or pushed permanently out of consciousness because we find them threatening. Some experiences, such as traumatic events of abuse in childhood, must also be pushed out and repressed because they are too upsetting. They evoke feelings of helplessness and harm that the conscious self cannot tolerate. Other feelings that end up in the unconscious have to do with instincts, natural drives toward such things as sexual pleasure.

- Psychology is associated with more recent developments in the sciences of the mind. It is less concerned with the unconscious and more concerned with cognition, with how the conscious mind works. Cognition is our primary way of engaging with the world; it allows us to make sense of what we see, to process and categorize sensory information, and to develop concepts for understanding our experience. Cognition can be brought to bear on the self in order to make it more healthy. Cognitive therapy trains patients suffering from various personality disorders such as narcissism or manic depressive illness to gain control over their mental processes in order to guide them toward a more fulfilling way of leading their lives.

- An important school of psychology grew up around the notion of "object relations." Object relations psychology is concerned with how our sense of self forms and is built up through our relations with significant caregivers ("objects"). Important issues include attachment and separation, as well as the boundaries of the self as it relates to others.

- Our selves are complex, and they are not what they appear to be. Our conscious awareness is only part of what our "self" is. Our past, our personal history, is crucial in determining what we are, yet it exists for our consciousness only as fragments of memory. The practice of psychoanalysis aims to recover the past that has been most influential on the current self. By making us aware of how past events and relationships have shaped us, it allows us to take control of things that might have control over us because we are unaware of how much influence they exert on our current behavior. A boy's fear of his father's violence or his mother's erratic emotional care at age 4 might affect his behavior at age

34. By becoming aware of that influence, he might be able to diminish its effect and might be able to lead a psychologically healthier life, one fully lived in the present rather than the past. The past also lives on in us in the form of wounds inflicted or strong feelings experienced. Memory is often just another word for "scar." The presence of the past in us can be quite negative, as when victims of traumatic events such as incest cannot escape what happened to them. They may not be able to recall the event, but it had such an impact on them and acted with such force on their psyche that they "act out" or behave in ways that are harmful to themselves. They repeat the traumatic wound because they have not come to terms with it. As a result, they are not able to lead fully successful lives.

Major Terms

Conscious/Unconscious   "Conscious" and "consciousness" refer to your awareness of yourself and of the world – your "thought process" as you move through any day. Consciousness consists of a mix of perceptions (what one sees around one as one experiences life), of purely mental events called "thoughts" (such as "I hope I can remember the names of the major political parties in Russia for the history exam. Those parties are …"), and emotions (such as the anger one feels when someone treats one unfairly). The "unconscious" refers to two things in psychology and psychoanalysis. The first derives from its use in recent cognitive psychology, and that means the mental processes that are just beneath conscious awareness. Some of the more interesting have to do with prejudice. We may not be aware of implicit or unconscious prejudices against others (especially other racial groups), but they are revealed in tests that show how they shape our choices and thoughts. In other words, we are not all aware of something that is part of "us" and that makes us react in certain ways to other people. The second meaning of "unconscious" derives from psychoanalysis, where it refers to the part of the mind that is unavailable to consciousness. The unconscious contains simple yearnings and desires such as "I hope I do well in the exam" or "I hope he loves me." But it also consists of repressed feelings and ideas that the conscious mind cannot tolerate (such as a memory of abuse in childhood). The content of the unconscious usually gains expression indirectly in our behavior and in mental processes such as dreams where the censorship the conscious mind usually brings to bear on the unconscious is not at work. Simple yearnings such as "I hope I do well in the exam" might take the form of a dream about success in running a race. But abuse in childhood, which leaves scars on the unconscious mind, can produce unhealthy behavior such as promiscuity or uncontrolled gambling or recklessness at work. The move from unconscious to consciousness often follows the path of displacement. A yearning or a need does not express itself through some direct means; instead it seeks out an alternative path that conceals the true nature of the desire or the need. Instead of asking for intimacy and affection, which would address our emotional needs, we seek out multiple sexual partners. A fear of failure, rather than taking the form of words that might make us appear weak, instead appears in a dream in displaced form (shifted onto something nearby) and takes the form of a fantasy of enormous success. Such displacement of a desire for one thing onto a desire for another makes the interpretation of mental activity tricky. What appears to be one thing is often another.

Attachment/Separation   Psychology is concerned with the self and its relations to the world around it (the self's "objects"). The self in this view is largely a conscious cognitive process. Emotions are part of cognition, although they are fueled by energies that lie deeper within the self. One of the principal areas of concern in psychology is the relations of the self to others. Such relations begin early in one's life, with one's relations to parents and siblings, but especially to parents. From such early relations emerge the skills and abilities that allow one to relate to others later in life (but often also the wounds and scars that prevent one from relating well to others). In the normal course of development, one begins with attachment to one's caregivers, and as one grows, one learns to separate from them and to achieve an independent existence. From the initial merger with attached others grows a capacity for building boundaries between oneself and those others. A boundary is predicated on and creates separation from the other. For some psychologists, such boundaries between one's self and one's "objects" are achieved by learning to take the world around one as an object of cognition. Instead of being immersed in it, one separates oneself into an independent unit of one's own. One does this through the construction of cognitive images or mental representations of the world. If one can represent the world around one in one's mind as an object of the self rather than as part of the self, one is separate from it. Failure to achieve such a separate unity or identity can lead to anxieties in later life regarding attachment to others. One can be overly aloof and unempathetic in relationships or one can be overly clingy and dependent, or one can be somewhere in between.

This school of thought posits an ideal of mental health that consists of secure and happy separation from others that permits one to have good relations with them that are not characterized by either excessive aggression or excessive yearning for attachment.

Identity/Identification   Identity refers to the self, especially to its separate existence on its own apart from relations with others. A self-identity is always complicated of course by relations and situations and social roles, things on the outside that affect what one is on the inside. Nevertheless, the personality one has apart from all of those things is a thing in itself – a way of thinking and feeling, a collection of experiences and memories, a disposition to feel and act in certain ways, etc. Both psychology and psychoanalysis use the word "identification" to talk about the self. In psychology, identification refers to the way we mold who we are by imitating those around us as we grow up. Often our parents offer ideal models of behavior for us, and we seek to imitate them by modeling our behavior on theirs. We identify with them, and that means our identity is constructed in part by imagining we are someone else or by making within ourselves an image of that other person that then serves as an ideal model for our own behavior.

Ego/Id/Superego   Sigmund Freud, the inventor of psychoanalysis, divided the mind into components. The ego is our conscious self. It maintains contact with the external world and acts as a censor against impulses from within that might be at odds with the rules, norms, and mandates of that external world. The id is the unconscious, but it is also the name for our own "it-ness," our belonging to physical nature, especially to the world of instinctual drives for survival and satisfaction. We all seek pleasure, Freud believed, and often that drive is sexual (the libido, he called it). The monitor in our selves that supervises the drives and keeps them in check is the super-ego, which also is our conscience, that in our self that maintains a sense of right and wrong, acceptable and unacceptable behavior.

Neurosis/Psychosis   What constitutes illness in psychology is different from what it is in psychoanalysis. Freud's version of psychoanalysis distinguished between neurosis, which was a conflict within the self between the conscious self or ego and the unconscious that could not be resolved and that resulted in symptomatic behavior, and psychosis, which consisted of a complete break with reality and a retreat into fantasy and disordered cognition full of fear, anxiety, and projection. In modern psychology there

with one's mother. At the base of the self is the initial loss of the mother that creates a "lack" that can never be restored, and human life consists of a deluded quest to do so. All our desires reach back to that earliest moment of attachment and loss in an attempt to find a satisfaction akin to the happy glow we felt in that initial moment of unity. We pursue a chain of possible fillers that are like signs pointing to something without ever delivering it. The sign is itself a token of the absence of the thing desired. All our yearnings are thus fruitless, in Lacan's eyes, attempts to reach something both in the future (of desire) and in our personal past (the original unity with the mother) that cannot be attained.

Lacan's work gave rise to an interesting strand of film criticism that combined Marxism with semiotics. According to this argument, capitalism fosters an ideal of individual selfhood that is conducive to a society organized around competition for scarce resources. This ideology stands in the way of organizing society differently so that resources would be distributed more equitably and equally. The experience of viewing a film, according to this theory, provides us with a feeling of plenitude and pleasure that is so appealing because it retroactively restores the lost sense of imaginary unity with the mother. The initial separation that leaves us all basically unhappy and desirous of surrogates to fill the breach in our beings – surrogates that capitalism happily provides in the form of endlessly cycled new commodities that we buy for pleasures that really deny us the true happiness that a fairer and more equitable society would provide – is thus welded cinematically so that the breach is healed, at least in fantasy.

Psychoanalysis was displaced by psychology in the middle of the 20th century. Psychology was less concerned with the relationship between consciousness and the unconscious or with the urge of the instinctual drives toward satisfaction, and more concerned with the behavior of the self in the world. Psychology concentrated on the relations between the self and its "objects," which could be anything from an important person such as a mother to an inanimate thing such as a teddy bear. We humans interact with the world as we grow and mature, and through those interactions we develop selves that are either healthy and well-functioning or unhealthy in a variety of ways. A healthy self is one that functions independently of others while yet being able to relate to them as separate entities without excess aggression or needy attachment. The concept of boundaries is important because the ability to construct boundaries allows the self to separate from caregivers and to exist as an adult within its own outlines.

The child's mind works initially through fantasies that it tests against the reality of the world around it. By internalizing or introjecting good objects and building up images of them inside itself (mental representations), it dispels the anxieties that plague a new being in the world. It also projects or expels outside itself onto bad objects feelings that disturb it. Cognition plays an important role in allowing the self to separate from the world around it and to develop as an independent entity. Mental representations, first of important caregivers, then of the world of objects, allows the self to build a boundary between itself and the world that enables it to grow. In this development, the self can come to rely on transitional objects that combine feelings of merger with the world and thinking that is more fantasy than reality (Calvin's doll Hobbes in the comic strip *Calvin and Hobbes* is a good example of this) with feelings of having a separate self.

Trauma is an important field of study within psychology because it is concerned with extreme examples of disturbance in the ability of the self to function properly. Often, this takes the form of a disturbance of boundaries, such that the person who has been traumatized has difficulty maintaining healthy boundaries with others. Trauma also poses a problem of cognition, since in trauma, the mind cannot take in what has been done to it, and the traumatic event remains as an experience that cannot be assimilated to consciousness. Traumatic experiences often etch themselves on the body in indelible ways that nevertheless are not possible to bring to conscious awareness. The mind defends against the pain by pushing it away. Often this defense mechanism takes the form of dissociation. Someone who is a victim of incest, for example, will imagine herself to be outside her body and to be observing what is being done to her from a perch on the ceiling. This mental ability to dissociate or separate from oneself allows one to pretend one is not experiencing something painful and traumatic, but it also prevents one from dealing with the event in a way that allows one to master it. Such failure often results in revictimization. Trauma victims often put themselves in situations that evoke the past trauma, or they victimize others in a way similar to what was done to them.

Recent developments in psychology focus on how the mind knows the world through cognition. All knowledge is a matter of bodies meeting other physical objects, and knowledge therefore is both nonmaterial (a matter of cognitive awareness that seems ideational though it is generated physically) and bodily (a matter of a body operating on the world through the brain or mind). When we say a work of literature "moves" us (to tears, say), we are noticing what these new cognitive studies are about: the physicality of our experience of the world and of works of literature and culture.

Examples of Psychological Analysis

The study of literature and of culture under the aegis of Freudian psychoanalysis has been widespread. Scholars generally are concerned with two things – the way texts manifest the unconscious and the way writers document the workings of the psyche in human relations. Writers often both explore the psyche and manifest their own troubled psyches in such explorations. Virginia Woolf suffered from bipolar illness or manic depression. She ultimately committed suicide. In bipolar illness, the self veers from periods of euphoria and elation, in which manic behavior is common (writing or speaking a great deal, for example), to periods of depression that can lead to suicide. In her novel *Mrs Dalloway*, Woolf explores these two sides of her own mental illness.

The novel takes place in one day that begins with Clarissa Dalloway saying "what a lark! what a plunge!" She is preparing a party for that evening, and she has invited old friends from her youth as well as the important political colleagues of her political husband, including the British Prime Minister. Clarissa manifests clear signs of elation and euphoria. She is taken up in what she is doing; it is a "lark," as she puts, something that is great fun. Lark suggests a bird in flight, and she is like that herself in her mood throughout the day. She appreciates all that is around her, exudes good will and kind behavior towards all. She relishes elegance and genteel politeness. In addition to embodying the symptoms of the manic side of bipolarity, she represents civilization understood as a happy control over and compromise with unseemly urges or troubling feelings. All of that is pushed away to keep the appearance of gentility intact, much as Clarissa assigns the care of her daughter to another woman. We learn later that Clarissa has made compromises throughout her life, giving up an earlier love with a woman friend and sacrificing a man who represents a more passionate sexual relationship than the one in which she apparently finds herself. Her husband is not someone for whom she feels great love or passion. Her whole married life is an emblem of compromise of the sort the self or ego makes as it represses desires and urges at odds with civility in order to survive in the world.

The other primary character, Septimus Smith, is a veteran of World War I who suffers from post-traumatic stress disorder. He is depressed, but in classic bipolar fashion, he also suffers from moods of ecstatic euphoria in which he feels connected to nature and senses the world around him in an almost painful manner. The connection to nature is an image that suggests

Septimus represents all in physical and human nature that is repressed by the civilization Clarissa embodies. He is all that lies just below the surface of the polite gentility she cherishes. He is directly expressive of his feelings and urges, and ultimately he kills himself as Clarissa watches, flinging himself onto a wrought iron fence in front of the house that is a metaphor of the boundary that sustains the civilized world and protects it from the natural urges that would disrupt its ideal of civility. If Clarissa's mantra throughout the day is "what a lark," his is "fear no more." He represents the release directly of all in us that civility makes us fear.

The novel thus explores the two sides of human psychic life. On the one hand stands all that protects us from our natures as physical beings, the animal within as well as the madness that would consist of directly expressed urges. On the other hand stands the natural world that is neither logical nor rational and that encompasses both the ecstasy of freely released drives and the ability to do harm to oneself and to others.

Elizabeth Bishop writes of a traumatic experience in her poem "Sestina."

> September rain falls on the house.
> In the failing light, the old grandmother
> sits in the kitchen with the child
> beside the Little Marvel Stove,
> reading the jokes from the almanac,
> laughing and talking to hide her tears.
>
> She thinks that her equinoctial tears
> and the rain that beats on the roof of the house
> were both foretold by the almanac,
> but only known to a grandmother.
> The iron kettle sings on the stove.
> She cuts some bread and says to the child,
>
> It's time for tea now; but the child
> is watching the teakettle's small hard tears
> dance like mad on the hot black stove,
> the way the rain must dance on the house.
> Tidying up, the old grandmother
> hangs up the clever almanac
>
> on its string. Birdlike, the almanac
> hovers half open above the child,
> hovers above the old grandmother
> and her teacup full of dark brown tears.

She shivers and says she thinks the house
feels chilly, and puts more wood in the stove.

It was to be, says the Marvel Stove.
I know what I know, says the almanac.
With crayons the child draws a rigid house
and a winding pathway. Then the child
puts in a man with buttons like tears
and shows it proudly to the grandmother.

But secretly, while the grandmother
busies herself about the stove,
the little moons fall down like tears
from between the pages of the almanac
into the flower bed the child
has carefully placed in the front of the house.

Time to plant tears, says the almanac.
The grandmother sings to the marvelous stove
and the child draws another inscrutable house.*

In order to understand what the poem is about, you should also read "In the Village," a prose piece by Bishop about a visit home by her mother, who was hospitalized for severe mental illness. (For a copy of "In the Village," see the appendix to Michael Ryan, *Literary Theory: A Practical Introduction* [Wiley] or Elizabeth Bishop, *Collected Prose* [Farrar, Straus & Giroux]). The visit was traumatic for the young Bishop, and both "Sestina" and "In the Village" are attempts to remember and to process the event. Disorder often produces a yearning for a compensatory order: notice that the poem is written in a prescribed poetic form (a sestina), which consists of six-line stanzas whose lines always end in the same six words. Cognition often is a way of bringing order to the world, of ordering and mastering it so that its dangerous elements can be accepted without feelings of anxiety. The sestina is a rather rigid kind of ordering device, and notice that the poem itself refers to things normally associated with order (a house) as being "rigid": "With crayons the child draws a rigid house." This suggests that Bishop and the child in the poem are trying to process an external traumatic event in a rather rigid fashion because the event is so painful. "In the Village" gives

---

* Elizabeth Bishop, "Sestina," pp. 123–4, from *THE COMPLETE POEMS 1927–1979* by Elizabeth Bishop. © Alice Helen Methfessel. Farrar, Straus & Giroux, LLC, 1980.

one a sense of why that event might have been impossible to internalize or integrate. The prose piece begins with a mad mother's scream that echoes throughout the town, provoking in the child disturbances of perception and defensive substitutions that ward off the pain the scream causes. Here in this poem, one sees a similar process at work. The grandmother talks "to hide her tears." The house they are in seems under assault from falling rain that "beats on the roof," and the emotional tone is embodied in the phrase "failing light." The grandmother tries to distract the child from her pain by offering a kind of ritualized temporal order ("time for tea now"). The almanac offers a similar image of emotional control that might help the child to contend with the traumatic event. It foretells things and thus controls the future. It offers the security of certain knowledge. These devices offer some help to the child, but it is her own activities, having internalized the lessons of the almanac, that lead the way to a successful processing of the trauma. The child draws a garden that allows tears to be planted and suffering to be converted into art. Through the ordering activities of art, painful emotional events can be dealt with, even though they may remain ultimately unassimilable to conscious awareness. That would seem to be the point of the final line. The "child draws another inscrutable house." "Inscrutable" suggests unknowable, as if Bishop were acknowledging that the ordering exercise of the mind in making art only goes so far. Trauma remains outside cognition.

Hawthorne's *The Scarlet Letter* is about psychological pain and how people deal with it. The most prominent emotions that Hawthorne describes in his characters are guilt, shame, and pleasure at others' suffering. Hester's experience resembles that of the child in "Sestina" in that she initially is characterized as being subjected to a shaming experience that is meant to instill a sense of guilt. The victim, however, is not so willing; she shrugs off the abuse and, rather than submit to shaming, she turns the badge of shame (a red "A" that she is obliged to wear as an emblem of adultery) into a badge of honor. She sews it so ornately that it transmutes shame into pride. What is meant to diminish the self in fact augments it. As her life proceeds, she does such good work in the community helping others that, in the end, she is recognized as being just the opposite of someone who is worthy of being shamed. She earns praise instead for her good works. Hester's life is a lesson in how the mind can work with painful and potentially traumatic experiences and successfully integrate and transform them.

The life of Arthur Dimmesdale, her partner in "sin," takes a different course because he is unable to successfully integrate his guilt. Rather than express it, he instead harbors it as a secret, and in the end it leaves its mark on his body. Hawthorne's conceit – that guilt when not expressed instead expresses itself mysteriously on one's body – in fact would seem to get at the reality of emotional experience – that it is bodily. When negative emotions are not turned into conscious awareness and dealt with and accepted, they can instead create physical symptoms. Dimmesdale's counterpart – Roger Chillingworth – also conceals a secret and does not express his emotions freely. If Dimmesdale's inability to contend with negative emotions harms himself, in Chillingworth, the same inability leads him to harm others. If Dimmesdale can be said to introject the hostility of his community against supposed "sinners" (Hawthorne does not really believe they are in fact sinners and calls what they did a "consecration") in a way that turns that hostility against himself, Chillingworth projects his animosity against Hester (his "bad object," the mother who did not love him enough) into the world and turns it against Dimmesdale, who is a substitute for Hester. If Hester recalls early experiences with one's mother for both men, Dimmesdale deals with that relationship healthily in the end when he rejects shame and freely expresses his affection for her. Chillingworth in contrast would seem to represent an unhealthy relationship with the mother, one that inverts positive affection and turns it into hatred and hostility. His merged life with Dimmesdale itself suggests a disturbance of personal boundaries and an inability to maintain proper ones between himself and the world.

The movie *Fight Club* is populated with Chillingworths, men who fail to develop a healthy relationship with early objects or caregivers and who as a result harbor resentment and anger against women. Like *The Scarlet Letter*, the movie is about mental illness, in this case a dissociative personality disorder, and it focuses on men's relationships to women, one of whom, Marla, provokes highly polarized feelings that recall a boy's conflicts about his relationship to his mother. The nameless main character's feelings are for animosity-driven separation, while in Tyler, the lead character's fantasy double, she provokes a desire for merger. That these feelings are part of the same personality is suggestive of how conflicted emotions can be toward the same person, especially if a relationship is not based on mutual separation and a separate identity. A sign of the failure to attain such an identity appears in the early moments of the movie when Jack is obliged to share emotions with Bob, a large man with breasts whose physical appearance and whose association with emotional attachment suggests a boy's early relationship with his mother. The lead character is clearly overwhelmed by this attachment, and the rest of the film is about his attempt to attain separation from the overwhelming maternal presence and the threatening emotionality that Bob represents. All emotions in this movie/novel are extreme, however, and the weightiness of the maternal attachment has to be dealt with through an excess of aggressivity that takes the form of "fight club," an all-male meeting place where men practice violence against each other. What the film displays is how a failure of appropriate care in childhood and a failure on the part of male children especially to develop a healthy sense of separation from their mothers results in the projection into the world of hostility against objects that recall the mother and the principle of care she represents. In the film, that hostility is directed at liberals whom conservatives accuse of caring overly much (like Bob in the movie) for others.

Citizen Kane is almost a textbook representation of a broken mother–child bond. In the sequence in which Kane is sent away from home by his mother, all the images suggest coldness, distance, and alienation between mother and child. It is snowing, and the mother appears heartless. She is associated with law and the signing of contracts, all highly impersonal activities. There is no warm affection anywhere in the household, and Mr. Thatcher, the banker who has come to take Kane away and to be his guardian, is dressed in funereal

Figure 7   *Citizen Kane*. Produced and directed by Orson Welles. 1941.

black. In one image, the mother sits in the foreground, and Kane as a boy is in the distant background – literally out in the cold. The stage set is designed in such a way that Kane is separated visually from his mother by door and window frames that serve as a metaphors for his actual relationship with her and for the impending abandonment of him by her.

Things to Look for in Literary and Cultural Texts

- Are the actions, feelings, and ideas depicted in a work signs of health or illness? If of illness, what kind of illness is it? How does it manifest itself in behavior or statements by the characters?

- How might the work itself be said to be a manifestation of psychological or emotional problems in the writer?

- How are relations between the characters depicted? Are they characterized by excess or obsession? What might such behavior be a symptom of?

- Does the work have an unconscious dimension? Are there aspects of the work that seem to arise from sources that are not conscious?

- How is the form of the work a way of dealing with psychological or emotional problems? Does the writer seem to be working on psychological or emotional problems in the work?

5

Marxism and Political Criticism

Major Texts

Karl Marx, *The German Ideology*
Karl Marx, *Capital*
Walter Benjamin, *Illuminations*
Theodor Adorno and Max Horkheimer, *The Dialectic of Enlightenment*
Michael Hardt and Antonio Negri, *Empire*

Major Ideas

- Capitalist society is divided into classes that are defined by the place each class occupies in relation to the production of goods for sale. Owners and investors possess accumulated wealth or capital that allows them to control the production of goods, while workers, because they have no accumulated wealth or capital, must give over their lives to labor in order to survive. According to Karl Marx, all humans are creative active beings. But under capitalism, workers' life energy, their creative power, is alienated from them in the course of the labor process. In such alienation, their life energy is taken out of them and turned into a thing, a manufactured good or a value that is then sold on the market as a commodity. The income from the sale of the good must be more than the cost of producing it, so workers' wages must be kept as low as possible for capitalism to function properly, for it to

An Introduction to Criticism: Literature / Film / Culture, First Edition. Michael Ryan.
© 2012 Michael Ryan. Published 2012 by Blackwell Publishing Ltd.

meet its goal of increasing the wealth of the owners of the means of production. Karl Marx argued that capitalism is therefore a species of theft: it steals the life energy of workers and turns it into the under-paid value in produced goods that allows them to be sold for a profit. Owners pay workers less than the value of their labor because manufactured goods must be able to be sold for more than they cost to produce. They must contain more value than the actual cost of pro-ducing them reflects. That surplus value over the cost of production is the origin of profit and wealth. In this labor theory of value, the source of capitalist wealth is the unpaid labor of workers. When Marx uses the term private property, he does not mean the clothes, gadgets, cars, and houses you own. He means the way in which the value workers as a col-lective group create around the world is converted into the private prop-erty of the owners of the means of production. Socially produced wealth becomes, under capitalism, private wealth. That, for Marx, is private property. When he said communisms would consist of the abolition of private property, he did not mean the commissars could remove you from your house and claim it for the state. He meant that workers would finally gain control over what they create and own it themselves. Writing in the middle of the 19th century, Marx saw this as occurring through the nationalization of large industry by the government. Later visions of communism saw the reclaiming of property by workers as occurring through workers' councils or small communes of producers.

- Marxism is also a theory of history. The same situation that obtains in modern capitalism – whereby a small group of owners and investors take advantage of or exploit the labor of others for their own private gain – obtained in the past. History is the history of class struggle, the fight between those with wealth and power and those whose labor sustains society. Ancient societies were communal, but as cities developed so also did a division of labor between those charged with growing food and making things and those charged with running society. Unpaid slave labor provided much of the work in ancient societies. In the Middle Ages, a class of unpaid serfs provided labor to sustain a ruling martial elite that maintained its power through force and through such cultural institutions as churches that preached the virtue of obedience. With the growth of trade during the Renaissance, modern capitalism became possible. Capitalism is defined by the investment of accumulated wealth in production that exploits workers, extracts value from their labor, and turns it into profit and more wealth for capitalists. The defining feature of all societies is the clash between those who own wealth and the means of manufacturing goods and those who own nothing but their labor power and must sacrifice their lives to the making of wealth for others in order to survive.

- The ruling ideas are always the ideas of the ruling class. Marx believed that culture plays an important role in maintaining the power of capitalists over workers (or of the party/state over workers as in modern China). A ruling idea is one that induces workers to voluntarily participate in their own subjugation because that idea makes the inequities and inequalities of society seem justified. In the Middle Ages, ruling ideas such as fealty and duty ensured that rebellion would not seem justified against economic inequality. In modern capitalist society, the idea of freedom makes the economic system seem a fair playing field where all compete equally.

- The capitalist economic system conceals the fact that it is exploitative from workers. Commodities or goods sold on the market appear to be things without any labor in them. The fact that they are sold and produce profit and wealth seems magical. This concealment of the origin of wealth is called commodity fetishism.

- Marx used the dialectical method he learned from the German philosopher Georg Hegel to pierce the apparent reality of capitalist society and to unfold its inner workings. The apparent reality of capitalism is that wealth arises magically from market exchange. The dialectic starts with what appears to be true – the surface of capitalism, which consists of goods for sale on the market. The method decides the surface reality could not be the full truth of capitalism since wealth cannot appear magically from the sale of goods unless they contain value that justifies the price they receive. Having negated the surface reality, the dialectical method then breaks that reality down into its component parts, and those are capital and labor. The dialectic consists of seeing things in dynamic relation to one another. In this case, capital depends on labor to make things, while labor depends on capital to pay wages to survive. This dynamic interaction, according to the dialectical method, is what must produce capitalist wealth, not the sale of goods on the market. Having broken the surface reality of capitalism down and negated it, the method now reconstructs that reality and comes back to the surface reality with a new understanding of how it comes about. It is produced by the interaction between labor and capital that goes on behind the scenes of the capitalist market. And that interaction consists of the extraction by capital from labor of a surplus value over the cost of producing goods.

- The dialectical method also works historically. The dialectic was originally a method of reasoning (Socrates is human; all humans are mortal; therefore Socrates must be mortal), and it works logically and through necessity. One premise must follow the others. Hegel and Marx both felt it applied to history and thought societies developed logically and through necessity from one form to another that was more complex. The dialectic works by locating a contradiction between a specific statement of fact (Socrates is human) and a general or universal statement (all humans are mortal). It then resolves the contradiction by combining the specific and the general statements together. Marx felt that the inherent contradiction in capitalism between labor and capital would eventually have to be resolved in favor of the more general premise (workers far outnumber owners and labor is a universal feature of life while ownership under capitalism is increasingly partial and limited to a minority). He felt that workers would finally lay claim to the product of their labor and take over the means of production in a nationalized socialist economic system.

- Literary and cultural works should be studied for how they manifest the tensions or contradictions that are inherent to capitalist society. The central contradiction is between the interests of workers and those of capitalists. Those works often collude with capitalism and conceal its operations behind diverting entertainment. But they also often put on display problems with the capitalist system of production. Culture is also considered a battleground by Marxist critics. Certain kinds of literature and film strive to break the kind of consciousness capitalism fosters. Other literary and cultural works argue in favor of sustaining inequality.

- All works of culture are made in social contexts that are fractured by political differences. Those differences manifest themselves in cultural works in various ways. In a fictional story, the choice of who is villain and who hero is a value judgment that often has political implications and resonances. In a modern conservative film such as *Iron Man II*, the businessman is heroic while the representatives of government – the nemesis of American business in real life – are portrayed as inept and corrupt. In a liberal film like *Avatar*, in contrast, the corporate businessman has bad values while the victims of corporate greed are depicted sympathetically.

Major Terms

Exchange Value/Use Value/Surplus Value   When workers work to produce things to be sold on the market in a capitalist society, they do so because the things will be useful to someone. Those things have use value (or utility). Once those products enter the market to be sold, they acquire exchange value. They can be traded for a certain amount of money. To be sold for a profit, they must be worth more on the market than the value put into them by labor and raw materials. They must contain surplus value. According to Marx, that surplus comes from paying workers less than the value their labor puts into manufactured goods (what Marx called "commodities").

Ideology   Ideology is the term for ideas or ways of thinking that foster belief in and support for social systems such as capitalism that benefit only a few people in a society, are organized around an unequal distribution of resources, and require that the coercion needed to maintain the system appears other than what it is. For Marx, ideology is "the ruling ideas of the ruling class."

Dialectic/Determination   Dialectic is the method of philosophy practiced by Georg Hegel and Marx. For both Hegel and Marx, something's identity, what it is in itself, is shaped or determined by other things to which it is related. The method of analysis thus moves from one thing to another to which it is inherently related (as "quantity" makes sense only as distinct from "quality") until an entire whole or "totality" is analyzed completely. Such analysis is concerned with the way one specific thing presupposes the existence of another thing in order to be what it is. A court of law, for example, is a specific concrete thing, but it presupposes a universal idea of justice in order to function. Its specific identity depends on something else. That something else helps to determine what it is. Dialectics thus emphasizes the relations between parts in a whole. It usually moves from very specific things to other things that are more general or universal until a point is reached where the necessity of both the specific and the general in order for there to be a whole is comprehended. A political system thus is both determinate institutions such as legislatures and universal ideas such as rights, and together they form an interdependent whole.

Summary and Discussion

Political criticism notices how literature and culture are about some of the major issues that divide us from each other – class or economic inequality, differences of power and prestige, the violation and mistreatment of others, domination by the powerful over the powerless, and the like. Most modern societies are divided between liberal and conservative groups, and culture is often a battleground for them. Liberals promote progressive change directed toward greater equality, conservatives the preservation of an unequal economic order. Conservatives ensure protection to the powerful and those who have succeeded in accumulating social wealth, while liberals seek to even the playing field between parties and to bring about a degree of fairness. Liberals reach beyond themselves to help others; conservatives devote themselves to self-interest. Conservatives rouse the masses for xenophobic agendas based on fear and hatred of minorities, while liberals seek to create rules and regulations for protecting everyone from unjust violation by others or by the state.

Writers often have political allegiances. F. Scott Fitzgerald and Orson Welles were both Marxists. Fitzgerald writes critically of the wealthy in *The Great Gatsby*, a group he portrays as casual, amoral exploiters of others. Orson Welles, in *Citizen Kane,* does something similar. Charlie Kane is portrayed as self-indulgent and profligate, a man essentially without ethical values. A conservative writer such as Ayn Rand, in contrast, depicts the striving capitalist individualist of *The Fountainhead* as heroic and superior to others, and she writes critically of socialism. Conservative filmmaker Francis Coppola does something similar in films such as *The Godfather* and *Patton*, in which great leaders are celebrated and, implicitly, democracy is denigrated. Conservatives favor authoritarian rule over the dangerous tendency of democracy to swerve toward egalitarianism, and that preference is very much evident in Coppola's films.

Conservatives and liberals clearly see the world through the lenses of differing belief systems or ideologies. Where liberals see individuals as connected to others in a web of relations that make accountability, responsibility, and mutual care important values, conservatives see individual self-interested atoms clashing in a combative economic arena.

Liberals see a world with defects that can be remedied by government; conservatives see a world whose traditional customs are inherently virtuous and oppose government when it is an agent of progressive change.

Ideologies in this sense are coherent belief systems that enable participants to understand the world in a certain way that coheres with how other holders of the ideology see the world. Ideologies in this sense are communities of meaning. However consistent they may be in themselves, they are not stable over time. Conservatives in England and North America used to believe in a strong government role in economic life. But with the advent of democracy, government became available to everyone, and its power could be used against conservative economic interests. As a result, conservatives switched ideology, favoring instead the ideal of freedom from government interference as a way of safeguarding the economic power of the wealthy elite.

When a particular group achieves economic and political dominance in a society, its ideology tends also to become dominant. It is difficult to see this in the short term, but over the long term it is more evident. Ideology in this sense means "the ruling ideas of the ruling class."

During the Middle Ages prior to the Renaissance in western Europe, a violent group of lords declared themselves to be a nobility with the right to rule a large peasant class of agricultural laborers. They promoted ideas such as fealty, honor, duty, chivalry, and obedience that made their rule seem justified. After the Renaissance and after the emergence of an urban commercial social class of merchants, traders, and small manufacturers that displaced the landed nobility that had ruled during the Middle Ages, ideas such as liberty and equality became dominant. They allowed the new ruling class to justify its position of power.

Social groups in dominance cannot rule by force alone. It would take an enormous effort of policing, torturing, intimidating, and killing. It is much better to convince the subordinated population that dominance is good for them or is so fixed a part of reality that it could never be changed. In the Middle Ages, the easiest thing was to say it was divinely ordained. A second meaning of the word "ideology," then, apart from "a consistent body of beliefs about the world," would be the ideas that allow one group to dominate a society by making such rule seem just, right, reasonable, natural, and, in some instances, perfectly divine.

Ideas constitute reality in that our experience of the world, our conscious awareness, is shaped by the ideas we hold in our minds. If you as a westerner encounter a Middle Eastern Arab, say, and if you see him through the ideational lens "terrorist," you will see him differently than if you were to perceive him through the lens of a more nuanced term or idea such as "Lebanese merchant" or "Iraqi school teacher." Our perceptual categories make what we see as much as do the objects we are looking at. When we see, we record reality, but we also paint it, mixing the coloration of our ideas with the objects before our eyes.

If those with social power control, as they often do, the production and circulation of ideas in a society, then they also control how that world is seen or known by its inhabitants. They control perception. As a result, the inequalities of station and of resource allocation that seem inevitably to attend the domination of one group over others will be perceived in ways that serve the interests of those in dominance.

The Renaissance that ended the Middle Ages was made possible by conquest and trade, but it was also made possible by new ideas that changed how people perceived the world around them. Merchants and crusaders brought back to Europe books and ideas from the Middle East that transformed the culture. The Roman Church was no longer the only source of ideas. Political criticism that takes its cue from Marxism is sensitive to how changes in culture and society are often brought about by changes in the economy. The trade that contact with the East made possible also allowed a new class of merchants and traders to supplant the rural nobility as the dominant social group in western Europe. With their ascendance came the circulation of new ideas that reflected their values and beliefs. In the Middle Ages, peasants believed that their lot in life was in fact ordained. With the rise of the merchant class to dominance, the nobility, their ideas, and the world those ideas held in place faded from view and were replaced by ideas such as mobility and equality. Dominant ideas usually cease to have a hold on people when others can mock them and get away with it. At the same time that Protestantism challenged the Roman Church, a French writer, François Rabelais, wrote books such as *Gargantua* that mocked the Roman Church's values, institutions, and practices, while a Spanish writer, Miguel de Cervantes, mocked the values and ideals of the nobility in *Don Quixote*. Rabelais was remarkable as well for writing in language that peasants could understand, their own vernacular French instead of the Latin the Roman Church favored. In this way, ideas could circulate more broadly and not be the monopoly of a ruling elite.

The merchants who were made wealthy by trade were not content to obey the Roman Church or to let a group of lazy nobles lord it over them. They demanded and got forms of government that allowed them to have some say in how society was run. They needed rules that suited their economic interests for one thing. And they wanted the nobles to stop interfering with trade and to stop using violence against them to maintain their rule. A new idea began to emerge – "liberty" – today we call it "freedom." It meant, among other things, that people had rights that could not be abused by violent lords. They were free to do as they wished. They also did not have to accept their lot in life. Destiny was no longer thought of as being ordained by God or by anyone else. Obedience to the church was no longer considered a virtue that guaranteed access to heaven. Those ideas went by the wayside as new secular forms of knowledge made it possible for people to think for themselves outside church orthodoxy. The old feudal economy was based on the idea of fixed stations in life – nobles at the top, peasants at the bottom. There was little in between. The new capitalist economy that supplanted the feudal one made mobility up and down the ladder of wealth possible. Another new idea was equality. Now everyone, rich and poor, had the same political and legal rights. They also had an equal chance of advancing themselves economically simply by being inventive, working hard, and adopting certain virtues such as frugality, thrift, and industry. No idea of fixed stations kept one in one's place. A new literary genre came into being called the picaresque novel (*Lazarillo de Tormes*), which concerned freedom of movement through geographic and socio-economic terrains that were barred from passage and obstructed from view just a few centuries earlier in heroic feudal romances such as *The Song of Roland* or the Arthurian legends.

The new ideology of freedom resembled the previous one based on fealty in that it legitimated an arrangement in which one group dominated society. The capitalist class, as Marx called it, consisted of people with accumulated wealth who owned what he called "the means of production" – the factories, corporations, businesses, and banks that made up most of economic life in the new post-medieval social order. The peasants who moved in masses to the cities to work for the new merchant class no longer had land on which to grow food, and they had no accumulated property. All they had to trade was their labor. So they were at the mercy of the merchants and had to accept low wages in return for their work. The result did not, at least initially, before a broad middle class came into being, look all that different from the Middle Ages. A lower class did all the work while an upper class extracted all the wealth for themselves. "Freedom" opened up all sorts of possibilities for those with talent, but it also began to seem like a false promise or a lure of some kind, a way of duping those who really did not benefit much from it into believing in an economic system that benefited others much more than themselves. For talent usually needed capital to thrive, and capital, simply by virtue of how the system worked, usually accrued only to those who already had some of it to invest. Otherwise, all one could do was work for wages that barely allowed one to survive physically, and that seemed much more the common lot. Only a rare few had both talent and capital to allow them to avoid the wage labor trap. Freedom was not equally distributed across the new post-medieval population.

The new form of society that capitalism brought about soon was the topic of literature. Late 18th-century novels such as Fanny Burney's *Cecilia* dealt with problems created by money or the shortage thereof, and as one moves into the 19th century one encounters more writers such as Balzac, who made the way traditional human relations were perverted by money central to his fiction. Victor Hugo wrote a hugely popular novel, *Les Misérables*, about how poverty and the spontaneous impulse to steal bread to feed a starving child can ruin a man's entire life. English novels such as Emily Brontë's *Wuthering Heights* began to be concerned with the differences between classes.

Another meaning of the word "ideology" is the way ideas like "freedom" operate in people's minds to ensure that they themselves contribute to their own domination. In this sense of the term, ideology is those practices of thought that ensure that we ourselves keep the locks on our chains firmly shut. We tell ourselves we are free even though we spend our lives working for others. A visitor from another planet would say we were patently nuts to think, under such circumstances, that we are "free." But so we continue to think. Why? The answer is ideology understood as those processes of thought that we use to convince ourselves that we are faring better than we actually are. Certain ideas that are essential to the successful operation of our economic system take root in our minds, and we use these ideas to convince ourselves that our lives are other than they are. By allowing ourselves to be indoctrinated by the ideology of "freedom," we learn to overlook our entrapment in a limited place in the economic system, and we convince ourselves that our range of life possibilities is much greater than it actually is. One is always "free" to go shopping, after all.

The cultural theory I am describing is usually called Marxism in honor of Karl Marx, the first thinker to conduct a critical analysis of modern economic life. He concluded that modern economic life works by paying workers less than they deserve for the value they put into the things they produce. Owners of the means of production (factories and corporations) keep that extra value for themselves. By so doing, they accumulate wealth. The resulting class difference keeps workers in their place, a permanent underclass in a state of permanent subordination.

Antonio Negri, an Italian Marxist theorist, thought that in reality workers have the potential to break the system apart at any time. They already over-produce goods so that owners regularly have to bring about recessions, a lowering of production brought about by a glut of goods and a fall in prices, to set things right and to make the system once again profitable. Workers are let go and reminded of who runs things. The number of goods on the market falls, and prices rise again. Once again, everything is right with the economic world. The natural potential in human labor to create enough to feed, clothe, and house everyone is restrained so that profitability for a select few can be restored, even as the well-being of the far larger majority is sacrificed. *Moby-Dick*, for example, is about workers on a sailing factory living under the cold, distant captain who appears disconnected from their labors. Melville describes their labors as creative and productive. They foster bonds between them of solidarity and community that are at odds with the distanced authority of the overseer, who keeps them in a subordinate position. Capitalism thus fosters community by bringing workers together, but it tries to prevent them from working together for ends that benefit the whole community rather than just the single owner and overseer.

Another group of theorists in this tradition have argued that we all yearn for the kind of world Negri describes – one in which all of our needs are fulfilled and in which we do not have to work long hours just to get by, work that makes a small minority in society very wealthy. Thinkers such as Ernst Bloch and Herbert Marcuse argued that literary texts bear yearnings within them for a utopian society, an ideal world of just, fair relations between people, where no one would exploit anyone else for private profit. The best works of literature negate reality as we know it and project instead an image of a better world. To negate here means something like "refuse to accept."

Theodor Adorno wrote a book called *Negative Dialectics* about all of this. He lived through Nazism in Germany in the 1930s, so he had direct experience of the violence that conservative defenders of capitalism are capable of. "Dialectics" is a philosophical method derived from Greek and Roman rhetoric. It originally meant a particular kind of thinking that proceeded from a simple initial thesis or proposition that was concrete and specific to its negation or opposite – a proposition that was general and universal. So one might begin with a specific fact such as "Socrates is a man," then move to its opposite – a very general, non-specific universal idea such as "all men are mortal." The dialectical method of analysis is finished when one follows out the logical consequence – "Socrates, then, must be mortal because he is a man and all men are mortal." That conclusion "follows" because it is necessary. If Socrates is human, he has to be mortal. Dialectical analysis sees things as necessarily connected to one another so that one presupposes the other and one follows from the other.

A German philosopher of the late 18th and early 19th centuries – G. W. F. Hegel – used the method to analyze everything from philosophy to society. He noticed that institutions embody ideas; one builds courts to realize in concrete reality a universal idea of "justice," for example. Specific concrete things like law courts thus exist because of general ideas; the two are dialectically intertwined; they presuppose one another. Justice makes no sense as an ideal if it is not concretely embodied in law courts, and law courts would not exist if there were not a general idea or concept "justice" that shaped what they are and how they operate.

Marx used the method to argue that one cannot understand what one sees before one's eyes in a capitalist economy – such as cars for sale in the marketplace – without thinking about them in terms of categories or concepts such as "capital" and "labor" and "value" and "profit." Just as what one sees when one looks at a court of law is only part of what it really is, and just as one must negate that sensory or empirical reality in order to grasp the idea behind it (in this case, the idea of "justice"), so also when one looks at the capitalist marketplace and sees a rich variety of goods for sale, one must negate that sensory reality and look at what it embodies, what ideas, concepts, and categories. For Marx, those informing concepts or categories were "labor" and "capital." A good for sale is embodied human labor that has been taken from the worker and turned into something that profits a select few wealthy investors, the owners of capital. It is, in other words, not what it first seems to be, and to understand what it really is one must negate that initial impression and move on to the social category and the underlying relation of social power that it embodies. A car for sale is more than a car; it is an intersection of two social categories – "capital" and "labor." And it is an embodiment of the exploitation of labor by capital, by the owners and investors who control the economic system and gain most from it.

To merely rest content with what you see is to be duped, because capitalism conceals its operations from its exploited labor force. Those workers do not wake up every day to read newspapers or hear news reports in the media that proclaim how well they have been exploited by a minority of wealthy investors and owners over the past several months, so much so that their labors have significantly increased the leisure enjoyment of that class of people. Instead, they see advertisements for cars that make them feel good about life. They are free to purchase whatever they wish so long as they are docile and contribute to the wealth and power of the minority of investors and owners.

For Adorno, negation meant refusing to accept the dominant prescribed reality of capitalist culture. Instead one should deny its validity and look for what has created it. Don't continue to shop mindlessly; ask yourself what you are buying, who made it, how much they were paid, who profits from the sale of the goods, etc. Negate and analyze further – that is what dialectical analysis promotes. Adorno and Max Horkheimer wrote a book called *The Dialectic of Enlightenment* in which they castigated capitalist culture for making our minds operate in routine ways by feeding us the same narrative formulas over and over again – the same songs, ads, movies, and TV shows. Capitalist culture succeeds by training us not to think critically about the world around us. We are fed rote cultural formulas and laugh tracks instead.

Examples of Marxist Analysis

The Scarlet Letter at first glance seems like a book about morality rather than politics, but in 1849, when it was written, morality was a form of politics, and moral debates in America were very much political debates. The two major political parties, the Whigs and the Democrats, were at odds over many things, including the proper role of government in regulating private morality. The Whigs, the conservative party, argued that church and state should be one; religious moral government should operate through secular government to impose a restrictive Protestant moral value system on people. They favored laws against adultery, for example, which punished women more harshly than men. Democrats, in contrast, considered moral legislation to be itself immoral. They felt God resided in nature, and natural processes should therefore not be interfered with. Natural passions were holy, not sinful.

In the novel, Hawthorne argues that the Whig ideal of moral government is wrong. It unjustly punishes Hester, who is depicted as someone with a natural bent toward charitable work for others. It seeks to impose rote rules on Pearl, who is depicted affirmatively and positively as a free spirit whose natural inclinations are imbued with virtue. And it turns Dimmesdale's life into an unnatural and perverse hell on earth. The only one who gains from the Whig moral scheme as it is represented in the Puritans is Chillingworth, and Hawthorne depicts him as a sick old man lacking in any real charity or empathy towards others.

The forest scene is pivotal in working out the novel's political position. In that scene, Pearl steps forward as the crucial figure in Dimmesdale's transformation. He has been cowed by his sense of sin and by the Whig/Puritan moral authorities, but he now decides to stand up to them and to reveal to all that a minister also experiences natural sexual passions and is as capable of sin as anyone. The Whig/Puritan ideal of moral government depended on the assumption that the "holy," the clerics who presumed to act as moral stewards of others, were sinless because they were closer to God. Hawthorne, in a typical Democratic argument, contends instead that divinity resides in nature and is available to anyone. This egalitarian argument countered the Whig belief that society should be organized hierarchically, with holy moral stewards at the top, providing moral government to those more distant from God. The novel's moral story is therefore very much a political story.

Hawthorne wrote at the same time as Marx, and what he analyzed and criticized in his novel was ideology, "the ruling ideas of the ruling class." The Whigs were the party of the economic elite in America at the time, the wealthy bankers, businessmen, and merchants who knew their power and wealth depended on maintaining social order by keeping the new immigrant working masses in line. Moral government was largely directed at this new population; it sought to regulate everything from prostitution to public alcohol consumption. By suggesting that natural desires should not be regulated by the government, Hawthorne took the side of the immigrant masses and undercut the justification for the Whig ideology.

Today, movies, television shows, and the news media do the job that novels and plays once did of maintaining social order by securing allegiance to an unequal social system by allowing only safe ideas that do not threaten the hegemony of the economic elite to get into wide circulation. Ideas at odds with power can be found on a small scale (Michael Moore's movies come to mind), but if those ideas ever became mass-produced or came to be held by the majority, economic inequality could not long be sustained. Alternative ideas are therefore always just that – alternative. The so-called "mainstream" constructed by the media and by entertainment companies continues to endorse the ideas such as "freedom" that secure allegiance to inequality, even when it runs counter to the interests of the majority. You will never see a television show in America devoted to exploring why socialism is a better idea than capitalism. The owners of the media are themselves wealthy capitalists; they would not stand for it. Occasionally, a filmmaker like James Cameron will accumulate enough to make an independent statement in favor of a socialist ethic in a film like *Avatar*, but it will be more likely to be the case in the mainstream that popular entertainment will endorse the values that sustain the economic system of entertainment. The *Iron Man* films, which appeared at roughly the same time as *Avatar*, are good examples of films with a conservative political agenda. At a time in history when Americans were torturing Arab opponents of the American business elite's interests, these films suggest that the problem in the world is that Arabs torture Americans. This misrepresentation serves the political function of justifying the torture of Arabs. In place of a vision of cooperative communities of the kind one sees in *Avatar*, the *Iron Man* films suggest that we should submit to the will of strong corporate leaders. Government, the embodiment of democracy, is portrayed as inept, and this is a way of suggesting that strong individual leaders are needed instead of democracy. The business elite is willing to provide them, the films suggest. This highly conservative vision coheres, needless to say, with the interests of those with economic power, and does little to unsettle the illogical justifications of economic inequality by the financial elite.

Hollywood attracts well-educated people with an interest in art, and such people often are liberal in political outlook. Orson Welles, the maker of *Citizen Kane*, was no exception. He fell out of grace with the industry in part for making a movie that supported workers. Like many liberal films, *Citizen Kane* argues against the conservative ideal of the superior individualist. Such thinking justifies allowing capitalists to do what they want to become wealthy in a world unregulated by anyone else, especially anyone with government power. Government is not an issue in the film, but the ideal of the superior individual is. Kane is like the hero of *Iron Man* in that he proposes to save the world on his own, using newspapers instead of weaponry. But the conservative ideal is the same: superior individuals should lead us. Welles portrayed this ideal as flawed because the person who imagines himself superior to others often is a self-centered megalomaniac who only cares about himself, his own needs, and his own ambitions. Such people lack a sense of principle, and they do not know how to temper self-interest for the good of the community or the will of the majority. In

Figure 8   *Citizen Kane*. Produced and directed by Orson Welles. 1941.

this image, Welles films Kane from below floor level so that his sense of grandiosity and self-importance can be captured visually.

Things to Look for in Literary and Cultural Texts

- How might the work be said to be political? Does it advocate a position in a public debate?

- Does it seem to support or advocate ideals, values, ways of thinking, etc. that distract attention from the inequities of capitalism or that conceal the true nature of capitalist society?

- Is the work critical and negative in regard to social inequality and injustice (under capitalism, for example)?

- Does the work seem to posit or propose an alternative to the world it criticizes? Is that alternative implicit or explicit?

6

Post-Structuralism and Deconstruction

Major Texts

Friedrich Nietzsche, "On Truth and Lying in an Extra-Moral Sense"
Jacques Derrida, *Of Grammatology*
Michel Foucault, *The Archeology of Knowledge*
Hélène Cixous, *The Laugh of the Medusa*
Jean-François Lyotard, *The Postmodern Condition*
Julia Kristeva, *Revolution in Poetic Language*
Félix Guattari and Gilles Deleuze, *A Thousand Plateaus*
Barbara Johnson, *A World of Difference*
Jean Baudrillard, *Simulations*

Major Ideas

- European philosophy in the early 20th century was dominated by the Phenomenology of Edmund Husserl. Husserl sought to find a way to make sure the mind was grasping truth with its ideas. He used the word "phenomenon" for the image that appears in the mind when we perceive something in the world. To make sure a phenomenon in the mind was absolutely true, Husserl believed that we had to purge it of all worldly connections so that the idea became a pure idea, something only in the mind. There it would become a purely formal entity without

An Introduction to Criticism: Literature / Film / Culture, First Edition. Michael Ryan.
© 2012 Michael Ryan. Published 2012 by Blackwell Publishing Ltd.

any real-world connections or content. It would be transcendental (untouched by contact with the world of everyday experience) and capable of being true as only a pure idea can be true (as, for example, in geometry, where the perfect triangle exists only as an idea).

- The dream of locating the grounds of truth in the mind's reasoning processes is an old one dating back to Plato, according to Jacques Derrida, a French philosopher who began criticizing this idealist tradition in philosophy in the mid-1960s. He noticed that idealists tend to base their claims on value judgments of which they are not aware. Truth is usually described as something morally good, alive, present, natural, authentic, and self-identical. It is distinguished from falsehood, which is morally bad, dead, not present, artificial, secondary or derived, and non-self-identical. Often idealists associate the voice or speech with truth and writing with falsehood because speech is closer than writing to the voice of the mind speaking to itself in thought. Drawing on Saussure's Structuralist Linguistics, Derrida argued that the voice was privileged in the idealist tradition because it was a direct signifier of the mind's true ideas, while writing was always considered to be an additional external signifier added on to the signifiers of mental speech. It was a signifier of a signifier and so less vivid, authentic, natural, present, original, and true. What Derrida called "deconstruction" consists of showing that this system of values is illogical. He demonstrated that the characteristic of writing – that it is a signifier of a signifier and therefore lacking in truth-value – was also a characteristic of all speech and all ideation. One cannot separate a realm of pure speech and pure ideas from the kind of articulation, differentiation, and spacing (signifier of a signifier) that one finds in writing. That is the case because of the principle of difference in Structuralist Linguistics (whereby the identity of any one part of language is made possible by its difference from other parts, as "hat" only has an identity inasmuch as it sounds different from "rat"). Derrida argued that the difference principle characterizes all ideation and all perception. Our ideas have identity only as they differ from one another. The same is true of perception. It is constantly differentiating in time and in space. If writing is bad in idealism, it is so because it is characterized by difference. As an external representation or image, writing differs from the true ideas associated with the voice of the mind in consciousness, which consists, according to idealism, of an immediate presence, full and complete in itself. Writing, in contrast, is a mechanism made up of parts that interconnect. Each part is determined by its difference from all other parts. But in order to even designate mental speech as superior to external writing, one must make a differentiation between the two. Even supposedly pure complete mental truth is made possible by differentiation. One could not know it as something separate from writing unless one could differentiate it. A more primordial process of differentiation has to be at work if the identity of truth is to be determined as separate from and superior to difference (in the form of writing). If difference characterizes all ideation and all perception, then the characteristics of writing (spacing, articulation, difference) cannot be rigorously distinguished from the characteristics of speech, the voice of the mind, and supposedly true ideas in the mind. The ground of truth is not presence but difference, which means the idealist notion of truth is not tenable – a presence grasped by the mind without any assistance from signification. And different grounds for our thinking have to be found, grounds that are less infused with prejudices about life/death, origin/derivation, authentic/artificial, presence/representation, speech/writing, etc.

- These "deconstructive" ideas had a profound impact on French intellectual life from the mid-1960s down through the 1980s, and they spawned a movement of deconstructive literary criticism in the US associated with a cluster of critics called the Yale School (Paul de Man, Barbara Johnson, and J. Hillis Miller especially). Derrida's work led to a questioning of identity and a questioning of the grounds of truth in philosophy and in our thinking in general about the world. Critics began to question the way the identity of women was constructed as different from or opposed to that of men. The identity of the literary text and of the author were questioned, and critics began to see how texts and authors emerged from broader "discourses," bodies of thought and writing that made certain texts possible and gave authors their ideas and ways of writing. Milton was a skilled poet, but he also embodied the discourse of Puritanism. In *Of Grammatology*, Derrida noted that a text supposedly refers to an author, but in fact, if the difference principle holds, then what the text refers to is something that refers to something else in order to be what it is. The flesh-and-blood Milton is certainly one ground that might arrest further reference, but Milton refers to Puritanism, which in turn refers to the state of affairs in mid-17th-century England, a contest of social forces and discourses. Reference can be stopped, but something will always be left out, and full truth in the idealist sense of a complete mental image will never be fully determined. There is always more truth than one thinks or can think.

- Derrida's work changed French critical thinking profoundly. Structuralist Michel Foucault began to investigate the way discourses operate apart from texts and give rise to them. Roland Barthes explored the ramifications of thinking about literature without reference to an author and in terms of the discursive codes that give rise to a text quite apart from the authorial referent. Julia Kristeva studied how certain radical texts deliberately explode standard versions of truth and of identity in progressive ways. Jean-François Lyotard argued that we never arrive at truth but always argue with stories, some of which are more convincing than others, a position echoed in the work of the American pragmatist philosopher Richard Rorty. And Jean Baudrillard suggested that representations and images have taken over reality and replaced it in the media, especially in the reporting of war.

- In the US, Derrida's influence is most evident in the Yale School, which argued that all texts are "unreadable" because the reference from language to world is so problematic. One never moves from language to things; there is always a mediating term. Reference always ends in an aporia, an irresolvable contradiction between the supposed presence of the thing a text refers to and the fact that to grasp the thing one needs language.

Major Terms

Analytic Philosophy/Continental Philosophy   English philosophy has been dominated by logic and language. Analytic philosophy is concerned with how we know and how we make sense with words of what we know. It is also concerned with the range and use of words to, for example, do things. Analytic philosophers emphasize positive facts rather than speculative systems of the kind one finds in continental philosophy (especially in writers such as Kant and Hegel). Continental philosophy aims for higher, broader goals – describing all of reality in philosophical terms (Hegel's dialectic, for example, which saw reality working in the same way as the mind).

Epistemology   The doctrine of knowledge; epistemology is concerned with how we know things.

Logocentrism   The Greek word *logos* means mind and word. "Logocentrism" is a term for the philosophical tradition that places an idealist conception of the mind at the center of the world. From Plato to Husserl, thinkers in this tradition assume the mind's own categories are the best standards of truthfulness. Logocentrism erases the mechanics of differentiation and signification that allow thought to occur.

Pre-Socratic Philosophy   The philosophers who wrote before Socrates in the sixth century BC in Greece were the first rationalists. They sought to provide rational explanations for the world. They sought the origin (*arche*) of things in first causes such as matter, or in a permanent, unchanging basis of being (*ontos*). Others were convinced that existence was characterized by flux and change.

Metaphysics   Literally, "beyond the physical," this branch of philosophy is concerned with ultimate things that are not specific to any particular science or discipline of philosophy. It became important as a term as a result of continental philosophy's recent turn toward anti-metaphysical arguments and ideas, especially in the work of Jacques Derrida.

Idealism   The philosophy, which originated with Plato, that believes there are ideas outside the physical world. For Plato, these were perfect concepts such as "Beauty" and "Justice" that one had to strive for in life, but the ideal form could never be fully realized in material existence.

Materialism   The opposite of idealism, materialism holds that all that exists is matter. There is no ideal world outside the physical one that "transcends" the physical.

Phenomenology   A modern philosophy that studies the cognitive conditions of knowledge. A phenomenon is a mental representation of a thing.

Pragmatism   The philosophy that thinks of the truth of a concept or idea in terms of its practical effects. How useful is an idea? If it is true, what effects or consequences ensue? Other philosophies seek to clarify ideas by analyzing their meaning in the abstract; pragmatism seeks clarity in examining the situation of ideas and their practical effects in those situations.

Deconstruction   A version of the critique of idealism, Deconstructionists hold that because identity arises from the differentiation between things, the principle of difference, rather than the principle of identity, is primary and generative of all that we can know. Rationalist philosophy holds that we grasp things cognitively by assigning them an identity (thus we know that "justice" is different from "corruption," for example; each has an identity). Deconstructionists note that no "thing" like "justice" can be grasped without differentiating it from other things. Difference, not identity, is the primary generative principle. What this means, however, is that the goal of philosophy – the fixing of the truth of things by locating their knowable identities – can never arrive at a final answer that takes the form of an identity. The final "truth" would itself be a differentiation. Deconstruction therefore is concerned with the instability of knowledge – its non-absolute character.

Foundationalism/Anti-Foundationalism Some philosophers believe there exist ideas such as justice and beauty that are absolute and true. They are universal in that they are the same everywhere. These ideas are called "foundations" because examples of each idea refer to the idea as its cause. We know that a painting is beautiful because the universally true idea of beauty is embodied in the painting. Such ideas are usually thought to be outside history and beyond the limitations of specific times and places. Anti-Foundationalists question these assumptions. They hold that for an idea like beauty to be universally true it would need to be so formal that it would become empty and useless as a category or measure. Moreover, ideas exist in practice in real time and in real places; they are historical, and they change with time and place or situation. That suggests that there is no one universal idea that is true everywhere. Rather than focus on universal ideas, we need to think instead about specific instances of a category such as beauty or justice and about its different meanings in specific situations. If foundationalism tends toward formal inflexibility, anti-foundationalism tends toward situational flexibility.

Summary and Discussion

Structuralism became Post-Structuralism in 1967 when Jacques Derrida first published his major works, such as *Of Grammatology*. Derrida's argument was with the illusion of cognitive autonomy which held that thought was a kind of spirit or ether that operated independently of the physical world in a parallel universe. A materialist would say that all thought occurs in a physical brain and is a physical process. Derrida was a Marxist and a materialist, but he was more interested in showing how idealism (the doctrine of cognitive autonomy) failed on its own terms. He looked therefore for ways in which an idealist philosophic text would uphold certain standards of truth but then be unable to sustain its claims. Texts declared one thing but described another. To notice this was to deconstruct the text.

Idealist texts declare that truth is something certain because it is a presence, something grasped in an immediate way by the mind. But whenever idealists describe that presence, they are obliged to resort to differentiations. And what that suggests is that difference makes presence possible. Difference, not presence, is the ground of truth. But of course difference does not satisfy the idealist criteria of truth because it is not a living presence in the conscious mind. It consists of articulation and spacing, a gap between things that are themselves articulations and differences. Endlessly.

Derrida was criticized for proposing a philosophy that said there was no certain way of establishing truth in crucial areas of human life such as ethics and politics. Other "post-modern" thinkers, like Jean-François Lyotard, took his ideas further and suggested that there was no need for grounds of truth because all we have anyway is language and stories. They help us live, but we have to abandon the hope that we will arrive at some absolutely true description of the world that is purged entirely of the uncertainty that attends all statements in any language. Others pragmatist thinkers argue that the most we can expect is to arrive at tentative descriptions of the world that then lead us to argue with one another until one description turns out to be more convincing than another. In politics, for example, conservatives and liberals succeed at differing points in time at arguing successfully for quite distinct visions of the world.

Derrida's work gave rise to innovative thinking both in literary criticism and in cultural analysis. Interest shifted from texts and authors exclusively to the discourses in which both were immersed. Investigations shifted from the ideas of the author or the meaning of the text to the rhetorical mechanics that made both possible. Literary texts came to seem less likely sources for universal truths; instead, attention was drawn to the values and assumptions contained in them (the binary oppositions such as presence/representation, authenticity/artifice, etc. that Derrida located in philosophy) and to the fact that texts are irreducibly rhetorical. One can never move from the tropes of language in literature to a real thing or a real presence of truth that the text supposedly delivers.

In cultural analysis, his work gave rise to investigations of the power of language to create realities. If language is a self-contained system for generating meaning and if one never moves from language to the real without the mediation of more discourse, more language, then language itself has an enormous power for generating a sense of reality. And that sense of reality can be variably accurate or inaccurate. Jean Baudrillard noticed that it is increasingly difficult in our lives to distinguish between artifice and reality. We live out lives shaped by consumer culture and derive meaning from the signs of that culture. The media gives us access to the world, but often images take the place of the real. War consists of stories and images we see on television, and we never can know the reality itself. According to Baudrillard, much of what we live in consists of simulations.

Marxists took issue with Post-Structuralism for two reasons. It suggested a new method of analysis that made the dialectical method favored by Marxists seem inadequate. And it suggested that truth might be difficult to determine, while Marxists felt that the truth, regarding capitalism especially, was easy to determine. Fredric Jameson suggested that Post-Structuralism was part of a new cultural moment called Post-Modernism characterized by a loss of depth in human perception and more of an emphasis on surfaces and representations. It was a symptom of "late capitalism."

The kind of thinking Derrida criticized is evident everywhere in Western culture, and it works in this way: the world is divided into a foundation of truth and a series of secondary and derivative traits or characteristics that suggest artifice, technique, inauthenticity, or insubstantiality. The foundation of truth is said to be closer to nature or to some ideal of presence that is substantial and real, while all against which it is posed is empty, artificial, technical, contrived, and false. The foundation is also closer to our own minds and our own living being, while what was false is portrayed as mechanical, technical, and non-living. Deconstructionists noted, for example, that truth in the idealist tradition was always linked to the voice of consciousness in the mind, while untruth was associated with an external technique – writing. It is hard not to prefer and give greater credence to the voice of the mind than to a mere written script that is a dead letter that might have come from anywhere and might be deceptive. The voice of the mind is immediately present; it must be the real thing, and it must be a token of authenticity and truthfulness. This way of thinking was designed to secure the idea that ideas exist apart from the physical world and that spirit is separate from body. But as Deconstructionists note, the idea of an ideal realm that is untouched by technical devices or processes of distinction in the material world is only possible to imagine using those very distinctions and devices.

Examples of Deconstructive Analysis

This way of thinking informs *The Matrix*, which distinguishes between the artificial, technical world of computers and the "real" and more authentic and true world of resistance fighters, who even wear "authentic" ragged clothing. Their authenticity is marked and in fact created by a representational distinction – between the corporate computer humans who look alike and speak alike, and the rebels who live in a world whose dirt and makeshift quality signal something more authentic or real. A Deconstructionist would note that this distinction is itself a device and a technique. In other words, the distinction on which the film bases its claim to be advancing the cause of a truer truth (the spirit world the rebels stand for, which is good because it is a living thing rather than an emotionless machine) is itself only possible if one uses technical distinctions that supposedly are not part of spirit. How can spirit exist if it can't exist without the very thing it claims not to be? If what "creates" the distinction between the spirit world and the material world is a distinction that, because it is a non-living, non-present contrivance or device, cannot be part of the spirit world, how can spirit be primary and foundational?

A deconstructive critique of *The Scarlet Letter* would focus on the way the concept of "nature" operates in the novel. It is like the concept of truth in idealist philosophy – something that is supposedly a manifestation of truth. Democrats at the time believed that there was a divinity in nature. Whigs, their political opponents, believed God was a distant being who shed grace on certain humans, but humans themselves could not connect with God directly except through churches. This way of conceiving of religion cohered with the Whig notion that a superior moral elite should direct society. As God was superior and inaccessible, so also the rulers of society should be superior. The Democratic theology emphasized the more egalitarian idea that anyone could atone for sins and get access to divinity simply by turning to nature.

Natural divinity in the novel resembles the transcendental ideas that Deconstruction criticizes. Nature is supposedly outside history in Hawthorne's conception of things. But divinity also informs and infuses the natural world. That of course means that the idea is incoherent. To be divine, nature must be both inside the human world and outside it.

Pearl has a similar function in that she is linked to spirit directly expressed in the human world, yet of course she is also human. Her truth derives from the spirit in nature that she embodies. Her natural spirituality is contrasted with the artificial and technical contrivance of the Puritan Catechism, which, like writing, is a mere repetition without vivid life or revealed religious truth. It is juxtaposed to the revealed truth of Dimmesdale's Election Day sermon, which has a powerful immediate effect on the democratic mass, who shout upon its conclusion. That sound is like the ideal of truth in the idealist tradition Derrida criticizes, which is often associated with the voice of the mind in consciousness. It is supposedly without articulation; it is living and whole unto itself, not itself because it is different from something else. But this value system is sustained by differences and articulations between ideologies, between the democratic ideal of "the people" and their will, on the one hand, and the Whig ideal of a supervisory government, armed with techniques of moral instruction, on the other. The democratic ideal of divinity revealed in nature is sustained and made possible by mechanisms of distinction and differentiation that pertain to a worldly realm of writing and repetition that supposedly lies outside of it.

Citizen Kane draws on similar ideas from the western idealist philosophic tradition. Leland is a representative of authenticity who is juxtaposed to Kane, who increasingly comes to be associated with falseness, inauthenticity, techniques of representation, and insubstantiality. The telling scene is when Kane celebrates the acquisition of *The Chronicle*, a rival newspaper. The sequence begins with a photograph of the *Chronicle*'s staff in the window of the rival newspaper. Notice that Kane is once again associated with a lack of substance. All we see of him is his reflection in the glass. The *Chronicle*'s staff are also characterized as lacking real substance. They too are only an image or representation. We then see a close-up of the photograph in the window, and, in voiceover, Kane describes how he wanted to buy the *Chronicle*'s staff and have them work for his newspaper. We think we are still looking at the photograph in the window of the *Chronicle*, but suddenly Kane walks in from the left of the frame, and we realize that we are looking at the actual *Chronicle* staff. They have been bought by Kane. The sequence is thus thematized as dealing with the way representation can take over from reality, and that is precisely Leland's fear regarding Kane – that he will allow the new writers to shape him rather than he them.

Figure 9   *Citizen Kane.* Produced and directed by Orson Welles. 1941.

Figure 10   *Citizen Kane.* Produced and directed by Orson Welles. 1941.

Their policies, which are so different from those of his newspaper, will become his own. The reformer may become a conservative, as indeed he eventually does. This corruption of values is depicted as an encroachment of representation on the real substance of presence, of falseness on truth.

Things to Look for in Literary and Cultural Texts

- Does the work assume a concept of what truth is? If so, what form does that truth take? Is it presented as the foundation of the fictional world, something that is beyond debate, absolute, and universal? Or is it presented as something more changeable, non-absolute, and contingent? Something "contingent" would be dependent on circumstances.

- What difference does the notion of truth in the work make for the events or lives depicted? Does the philosophical assumption of the work connect to other assumptions about, for example, morality or politics?

- Idealist notions of truth as something absolute and universal often are associated with nature. Does such an association appear in the work? Is the ideal of nature juxtaposed to characters, events, or institutions associated with all that is not natural – that is, for example, artificial, fabricated, simulated, or false? What are the implications of such distinctions in the work? Are certain characters portrayed as being better because they are closer to nature while those who are closer to non-natural artifice are portrayed as bad in some way?

7

Gender Criticism

Major Works

Adrienne Rich, "Compulsory Heterosexuality"
Diane Rubin, "The Traffic in Women"
Laura Mulvey, "Visual Pleasure and Narrative Cinema"
Sandra Gilbert and Susan Gubar, *The Madwoman in the Attic*
Luce Irigaray, *Speculum of the Other Woman*
Judith Butler, *Gender Trouble*
Henry Abelove et al., *The Lesbian and Gay Studies Reader*
Eve Kosofsky Sedgwick, *Epistemology of the Closet*
I. Morland et al., *Queer Theory*

Major Ideas

- Culture provides a record of how women and men have lived and been obliged to live over the course of human history. I say "obliged to live" because Feminist scholars argue that women's lives have been limited by constraints placed on them by male-dominated societies. They have been prevented by law from working in the professions and were assigned secondary roles such as "home-maker," despite being as talented as men at more public occupations. That has begun to change, but men largely control political and economic life around the world, and in some societies women are still obliged to wear a veil, to sacrifice work, education,

An Introduction to Criticism: Literature / Film / Culture, First Edition. Michael Ryan.
© 2012 Michael Ryan. Published 2012 by Blackwell Publishing Ltd.

and career, and to marry while still very young to much older men. They are assigned secondary roles and secondary lives, and those roles are often enforced violently by such practices as burning and mutilation.

- Feminist critics and cultural historians study images of women in literature and culture, and they have found that women often are portrayed in either extremely negative or extremely positive stereotypes. Women are often seen as a threat to male power and potency. But they are also depicted as angels whose mission in life is to care for men. It is the task of Feminist scholars to rectify the imbalances of the literary and cultural tradition created by the rule of men over women. More men than women are represented in the literary canon. Feminist scholars draw attention to the works of women writers, many of whom have been neglected by scholars.

- Gender scholars also study how the identity of men is constructed through cultural practices and images over time. They focus on the ideal of masculinity and find that the images of strength associated with that ideal often carry in them anxieties about effeminacy and loss of power, and threats of shame and embarrassment. They also find that the qualities associated with masculinity are distributed across both men and women. There are masculine women as there are effeminate men. What this suggests is that the qualities and characteristics of the gender ideals may not be biologically rooted. It is possible that the characteristics and qualities of masculinity and femininity are either temperamental and personal historical (rather than genetic) or learned.

- The study of sexual and gender identity in literature and culture quickly expanded to include gay male, lesbian, bisexual, and transgendered identities. There is a strong strain in human culture of antipathy and animosity toward non-majoritarian sexual and gender identities. Laws have forbidden homosexuality in many societies. But many writers were, and are, gay or lesbian, and often their works reflect a hidden undercurrent in human culture.

- Queer Theory is the most recent iteration of Gender Studies. A more provocative approach, it suggests that heterosexuality is not a norm in relation to which the other gender identities and practices are marginal or minoritarian. Queer Theory assumes that all sexuality is infused with homosexuality and that there is no normative heterosexual center around which cluster various marginal identities. Evidence of queerness is everywhere in supposedly heterosexual culture, from male love in Hong Kong crime dramas to the emotional bonding in all-male and all-female sports teams. In ancient Greece, sexual relations between men and boys were considered a normal part of growing up for members of the aristocracy. This suggests that even apparently fully heterosexual people are capable of practices usually associated with homosexuals. Queer Theory thus assumes that no gender category is stable or normative. All are contingent and malleable, and those that appear natural are merely held in place and enforced by cultural constructions that require certain kinds of reproductive behavior of subject populations. A certain amount of conservative intolerance in culture prevents more people from acting on bisexual or homosexual impulses. The study of human culture displays evidence of those impulses. To queer a text is to reveal those impulses and to show that all gender categories are contingent rather than being derived from a natural ground that makes them immutable.

Major Terms

Feminism   Women scholars became interested in studying images of women in literature and works of literature by women in part as a result of the Feminist movement, the most recent iteration of which started in the 1960s. Social critics began to notice that the ideal of femininity in American culture especially had a debilitating effect on women. It portrayed them as weak and incapable; their only talents were domestic. Moreover, the feminine ideal limited women to being sexual partners to men. That was supposedly their goal in life. But culture, Feminist scholars found, is populated with examples of strong, capable women who played strong roles in human history. Scholarly work on the history of women ranges from that which celebrates images of female strength and accomplishment comparable to those of men to that which notices that women have often been associated with talents and abilities that distinguish them from men. Women have an identity of their own, according to these scholars, with particular psychological characteristics such as interpersonal connectedness and care.

Compulsory Heterosexuality   This term, invented by Adrienne Rich, describes the way women were forced, prior to the 1960s, to be heterosexual even if they were homosexual.

Patriarchy   Rule by men.

Gender Identity   Gender is the term scholars use to distinguish the cultural norms and ideals regarding masculinity and femininity from biological sexuality. We are born with a clear biological sexual identity in most instances, although a number of humans are intergender and combine traits. But we learn behavior appropriate to that biological sexual identity from culture. Gender is often described as learned behavior. Increasingly, scientists are challenging this distinction between culture and biology, and argue that all supposedly learned behavior is also biological. There is no separation between the physical world of genetic biology and another realm called "culture" where we learn behaviors that are foreign to our biological identities. Cultural ideals of femininity do indeed represent and apply to a certain population of women, but human sexual identity, apart from the biological binary of male/female, is multiform. Masculine women exist, as do feminine men. Cultural gender ideals therefore do not pertain to all men and women. One can be one thing physiologically and another thing in regard to psychology, temperament, and proclivity. Gender is a way of distinguishing the latter from the former. It allows for the possibility that someone might be physiologically a woman characterized by the same sexual physiology as a heterosexual woman yet be entirely anti-heterosexual and entirely homosexual or lesbian in orientation.

Difference   The idea of difference is associated with the claim made by some Feminists that women's identities are distinct in some way from men's. Usually, they argue that female identity is more relational and less characterized by boundary anxiety because girls do not experience the same need to separate from their mother as they grow up. They instead acquire an identity by emulating their mother, while boys must distinguish themselves from the person who is usually the primary care provider to children. Such separation fosters anxiety about whether or not the male child has succeeded in separating from an initial feminine identity that is so antithetical to the cultural ideal for masculine identity. Many men therefore experience anxiety about being seen has having "feminine" traits.

French Feminism   Quite distinct from Anglo-American Feminism, which focuses on recovering women's history and studying women's oppression, French Feminism concerns itself instead with describing the powers of women and of the "feminine" in Western culture. Women, they argue, are associated with the repressed underside of patriarchal philosophy and culture, the unformed matter on which all Western ideals of reason and social order are based. That matter makes culture possible, but it threatens the orders of that culture because it is inherently unformed and without identity; therefore it must be contained and repressed. The subordination of women's materiality is necessary for patriarchal culture, with its hierarchies, boundaries, and identities, to come into being.

Homosocial   A term used for same-sex social relations of the kind that are evident in the knightly culture of the Middle Ages or on board whaling and pirate vessels in the 18th and 19th centuries. It was first used by Eve Sedgwick, who criticized all male conservative political administrations such as that of Ronald Reagan in the 1980s who, despite their clear affective and affectionate bonds for each other, disparaged homosexuals.

Queer   The position that holds that all gender identities are unstable and contingent. All are social or cultural constructs. Sexuality is diffuse and indeterminate. Even so-called standard heterosexuality contains queer elements.

Summary and Discussion

Gender has been an especially important concern of literary and cultural analysis for the past half-century because of the emergence of the Feminist movement in the 1960s and the subsequent transformation that it brought about in the world. Traditionally, women had been assigned secondary social roles by men, who monopolized resources and power for themselves. And in some parts of the world that is still the case. But Feminism ushered in a new era in more modern regions, such that women now can occupy positions of power and can practice professions from which they had previously been excluded.

Feminism also changed the study of literature and culture. In the past, the largely male professoriate in colleges and universities had not taken questions of gender seriously and had not noticed that the way women were portrayed in literature and culture was often quite negative and in keeping with power structures that kept women in a subordinate social position. The cultural representations and the social reality reinforced one another. To challenge the cultural representations was therefore in effect to challenge the unequal status of women in the world. Were women really snakes, demons, monsters, witches, and castrators, as men had imagined them to be? Not really, but the images in culture, from the myth of Medusa to movies like *Fatal Attraction*, justified the application of force by men to women so that women could be kept under control. That fantasy of fear and violent defense made women's subordination in society seem necessary.

Things have changed, of course, and women now have greater access both to resources and to careers in most parts of the world. Literature by and for women has proliferated, as have films and songs. To study the historical subordination of women is a bit like studying slavery; it once was prevalent, but it is much less so now. Nevertheless, the way of thinking that in the past justified the subordination of women to men (e.g., in culturally underdeveloped parts of the world such as Saudi Arabia, where conservatism still reigns) still persists. Such practices as sexual slavery are also still widespread, and they fall disproportionately on women.

Why does patriarchal thinking persist even in cultures where liberal ideas regarding women's equality with men seem to have taken hold? It may be because the survival of a society based on predatory competition amongst its members depends on the fostering of values such as toughness, violence, dominance, and emotionlessness that have in the past been assigned to men. The patriarchal tradition allocated to women the roles of caregiver and housekeeper, even though the values of empathy, care, and self-sacrifice that such labor demanded were often alien to many women's temperaments and were to be found in many men's. It was probably simpler to assign social roles along biological gender lines even though the competencies for various tasks, from hunting or competing to caring and tending, were distributed across the two biological genders. But because the ancestral culture of patriarchy favored values associated with men, such as strength, independence, and competitiveness, and because those values are necessary for survival in a competitive society in which, despite all of its civilized modernity, failure can still mean homelessness, poverty, and starvation, men have a residual, if not always deserved, privilege. The ancestral cultural legacy makes it appear that they bear the traits necessary for success in a brutal world.

Or so the story goes. It depends in part on who is telling the story. Culture does not speak with one voice. More modern, more liberal sensibilities are likely to picture strong women such as Ripley in the *Alien* movies positively, while a traditionalist writer such as Michael Crichton is likely to picture strong women such as Meredith Johnson in *Disclosure*, who rapes a man, then torments him in the workplace, as a deviant monster.

Prior to the 20th century, women writers such as Mary Wollstonecraft (in *A Vindication of the Rights of Woman*) argued that women were oppressed by men. From the mid-19th century through World War I, a first wave of Feminism posed the question of why women had fewer rights than men and why they were excluded from public life. This critique of patriarchy occurred in books and in the streets. Suffragettes in England who argued women should have the same right to vote as men were imprisoned for their activities. The Feminist movement was reignited in the 1960s in a second wave that concentrated on the social status of women. Women were secondary to men in all respects, including access to power and to economic opportunity. These Feminists were especially critical of the way culture operated to secure women's oppression. Many male writers used misogynist images of women that designated them as sexual objects exclusively, or as dangers to men.

In literary and cultural studies, Feminist scholars began to study the history of women in Western culture. Women writers who had been designated as marginal in the male-dominated academy were given more attention and more importance. Issues of gender inequality became topics of scholarly discussion. Gilbert and Gubar, in *The Madwoman in the Attic*, argued that the images of women in Western culture conspired to make women authors anxious regarding their power and ability to write. Those images were either extremely positive or extremely negative; women had to choose between seeing themselves as angelic servants of men and children or as dangerous monsters whose bodies were repugnant to men. Women with autonomy, independence, or power were especially dangerous in the male-dominated cultural tradition.

Are women fundamentally different from men? The patriarchal tradition said yes in a negative way; women possess traits such as frailty, dependence, and emotionality that make them subordinate, and when they eschew that social position and those traits they become dangerous to men. But some Feminists embraced the idea that women are different in a positive sense. Some argued that women are more likely to be characterized by values such as empathy and care for others, although this position often seemed to mistake socially mandated and learned dispositions for natural ones. Others contended that there exists a feminine style of thought that is more complex and relational than the patriarchal one (which relies on simplistic oppositions between absolute categories such as authentic/artificial, true/false, tough/weak, independent/dependent, etc.). Feminine thought blurs the sharp lines between supposed opposites, seeing the way the artificial and the authentic are intertwined, for example. All models of male authenticity, for example, are dependent on a differentiation from artificiality to be what they are. No value exists on its own apart from the field of relations in which it is immersed and that give it its identity as a category. All thinking is to a degree feminine. It depends on relations. While the argument is a good one, it assumes relations are feminine rather than masculine, and yet many examples of supposed "feminine writing" are by men. Other influences, such as political attitude, may account for the distinction between thinking in simple oppositions and complex relational thinking.

French Post-Structuralism gave rise to a different strand of Feminism. It posited an ideal of "feminine writing" that was transgendered and that operated in accordance with the difference principle, which holds that identity is formed by relations between things that are themselves constituted by relations. There is as a result no possibility of a stable determinate identity in culture. Everything comes into being through its difference from something else. Women are not an identity of their own; they are merely made different by a dominant male culture, which lives in denial of its own constitution in difference, its own fundamental and essential relation, in its own "identity," to femininity. Certain writers notice this state of affairs. James Joyce, for example, in *Ulysses*, writes "as a woman" and breaks down the order of grammatical discourse to generate a new transgendered discourse that is "feminine" because it avoids the repressions of traditional male discourse.

Ethnic minority women took issue with the focus on White women's writing in Feminism, and an adjacent Feminist movement began in Ethnic Studies. Then lesbians began to criticize the focus on heterosexual writers in Feminism, and that served as the ground upon which Gender Studies arose. Gender Studies is broader than Feminism in that it encompasses gay, lesbian, bisexual, and transgender writing and concerns. It in turn gave rise to Queer Theory.

Gender is different from physiological sexuality. Most people are physiologically male or female in biological gender, but gender as a term in cultural analysis refers to the identity we attain apart from physiology. Men can be feminine and women masculine, but in addition, even supposedly "normal" mainstream heterosexual identity categories may, according to Gender Theory, be learned. The *Kinsey Report* found that most people have homosexual impulses at some point in their lives, but they nevertheless conform to the prevailing standards for heterosexuals and do not engage in homosexual sexual activities. That may be because normative heterosexual behavior is prescribed and learned. A society founded on reproductive heterosexuality may see a gain in repressing homosexuality in the population, and this largely unconscious process may work itself out through cultural prescriptions that mandate certain kinds of behavior for particular genders. The movies of the 1950s in the US, for example, are wonderful examples of prescribed heterosexual behavior. Homosexuality is occasionally playfully evoked, as in *Pillow Talk*, but then as playfully suppressed.

Gender is an important category because it emphasizes the role culture plays in shaping what we are. We learn at an early age to perform our gender, to act out the roles suitable to our biological sex. But gender culture is often at odds with biology. Some women are as strong and as independent as men, and some women love women as sexual objects and romantic partners. Such discrepancies draw attention to the cultural dimension of gender, the way it is a matter of conditioning that is at odds with biology. But one must also ask where such gendered cultural conditioning comes from and what biological purpose it serves. It is carried out in a patriarchal world anchored in biological imperatives that drive us toward survival. In such a world, it is mandatory that people behave in certain ways in regard to gender if the community is to survive. The patriarchal division of labor between male hunters and female nurturers resulted from such evolutionary pressures.

Does that mean patriarchy is "natural" and therefore obligatory? Studies show that women and men are equally aggressive, once one takes indirect or "passive" aggression into account, and studies have also shown that women, who supposedly are better equipped than men to talk with others, are not in fact better talkers. Both genders are equally able in terms of speech interaction. The same is true of mathematics, another supposed dividing line between genders. The patriarchal division of labor may have left a legacy in our dispositions, but it is not very noticeable. Given a chance, men make as good parents as women, and women make as good corporate executives. The nurturer/hunter role division may have been a matter of historical expediency rather than natural necessity. It apparently never made its way into our biological hardwiring.

While many cultural assumptions about gender difference may be prejudices generated by past patriarchal practices that once served communal needs that are no longer as pressing, some are nevertheless real: men and women have different bodies and differ in regard to such things as susceptibility to cardiovascular illness. Moreover, the culture of gender difference has bodily effects. Cultural practices such as exclusion can affect people physically. For example, women are twice as likely as men to suffer from depression. Why? The answer may reside in biological differences, but the difference may also be the result of cultural pressures – in this case, exclusion from fulfilled lives of the kind much more easily available to men in a society still operating with many patriarchal assumptions intact. Envy, anger, and resentment make us pay a second time for the traits that gain us exclusion from social resources and rewards.

The work of Judith Butler and Eve Kosofsky Sedgwick was especially important for Gender Studies. Sedgwick advanced the concept of "homo-sociality," which names the way same-sex bonding works in "normal" het-erosexual culture. There is a continuum between practicing homosexuals and the non-practicing, repressed homosexuality of the all-male bonded group. Here, it is helpful to evoke the example of societies in which dominant male groups actually not only bonded homosocially but also practiced homosexuality, such as ancient Greece. Butler argued that gender is learned. We strive to perform an ideal of either masculinity or femininity that is supplied to us by our culture. Because gender identity is a performance, it has no real ground or substance. Drag, which consists of people dressing up in clothes assigned to the other biological gender, is an imitation, but its success suggests that all gender is imitative. We all act what we would like to be in a gender sense. We strive to imitate a cultural ideal, and that is how our gender identity comes into being – in imitation of an idea. We strive to appear "natural," but the more we do so, the more we draw attention to the fabrication of gender by culture. Constant repetition of the ideal of either masculinity or femininity in our daily lives makes us ignore the fundamental insubstantiality of gender identity, its performed, practiced, and learned character.

More recent gender scholars have focused on the way in which the ideal of masculinity works to the detriment of women and of gender minorities. Judith Halberstam, in contrast, has argued for a progressive use of masculinity by biological women who have been denied images of self-empowerment. Simply because men have abused the ideal of masculin-ity does not mean it is without use to women seeking ways of strengthening themselves and expanding the range of possible identities they can occupy. Other scholars have focused on the body and advanced a concept of a materialist Feminism rooted in bodily life. The study of emotion derives from this strand of Gender Studies.

The principle of difference in Structuralism and Post-Structuralism has been extremely helpful to Gender Theorists. If all things have identity only through their relations to other things, then it is extremely difficult to isolate the identity of anything from the field of relations in which it is located. All identity is field-dependent. Identity is therefore characterized by indeterminacy and contingency. It is not a substance with an identity of its own that is clearly demarcated from other identities. It is hard to pin down, and when one does pin it down, it turns out to depend on something else that is itself unstable and indeterminate. Proponents of the transgender and the queer in Gender Studies latch on to these notions and exploit them to generate very useful new descriptions of gender. According to these scholars, there is nothing natural about gender. It is important to disrupt and denaturalize the reigning notions and models of gender identity by exploring such things as androgyny, butchness, female masculinity, inversion and perversion, and bodily transformation. Queer disrupts the normality of heterosexuality in particular, and of any stable gender identity in general. According to the difference principle, instead of identity there is always an in-between, and Queer Theory explores this as the "normal" reality of gender. Transgender is not a margin in relation to a center; it is what the center suppresses within itself in order to centralize and identify itself. Beneath the reigning norms of gender is a more fluid and indeterminate reality on which gender is built but which must be suppressed if gender identity is to reign as it does in human life. Exposing that norm-disruptive side of gender life is the goal of queering.

Recent Gender Theory therefore posits the existence beneath the reigning gender forms of a realm where genders mix and are less clearly distinct. It is characterized less by firm and clear oppositions between male and female, and more by a fluid blending of gender possibilities. Research has borne out the contention that many people do not fit easily into the prevailing male/female gender categories. Many more people than one would expect, given the ferocity with which the reigning gender categories are enforced, are inclined to experience homosexual desire at some point in their lives. That may account for why Greek culture was so easily able to adapt itself to institutionalized male–male love as an alternative to the kinds of male–female mating rituals found in other cultures. When the Greeks decided women should be relegated to the inner domains of the home and only let out infrequently, some alternative had to be found. That heterosexual men so readily took up sexual practices normally thought to pertain exclusively to homosexual culture or to modern prison culture suggests that the modern imperative that one must choose one sex-gender format over all others does a disservice to humans' biological potential. Most of us may be biologically male or female, but our gender identity contains many more possible permutations.

Gender is not only a feature of sexual identity and sexual behavior. It can also manifest itself in other ways, from style of speech to style of dress. Some scientists, for example, when they are criticizing opposed positions, especially those in other fields that are perceived to be less "scientific" such as the social sciences or cultural studies, use terms like "hard" and "rigorous" and "substantial" to characterize what they do. The other discipline is characterized as lacking rigor, or as being soft, or as proposing arguments for its positions that are now "in retreat." The metaphors of such a way of talking are often martial (that is, they derive from the language of war) and suggest a battle between manly men and their weak-kneed adversaries. Such discourse may be a matter of right ideas, but it is also patently gendered. It gives expression to biological urges to dominate as much as some forms of sex do. A similar gendering occurs in the way we raise children. We can encourage them to be whatever they wish to be from a gender perspective and allow their biological impulses to express themselves freely, or we can do what a mother I rode in an elevator with recently did when she said to her crying son, who was lamenting the departure of his "daddy": "Stop crying like a baby." She may have been teaching him toughness of a kind that her ancestral biological inheritance urged her to believe would be necessary for him to survive in a tough world, but she was also engaged in cultural gendering.

Examples of Gender Analysis

Shakespeare's *King Lear* was presented first to King James' court as part of a Christmas celebration. That court was described in a contemporary account as a haven for "catamites" or homosexuals. James was himself gay and kept a gay lover. One might expect that a play put on by one branch of London's gay underworld for the entertainment of another branch might have gay elements to it, and that indeed is the case. Unlike other plays of his that explore the gender consequences of cross-dressing, *Lear* deals instead with a stripped-down version of humanity. The king goes mad, encounters his thematic double, the noble Edgar on the heath, and takes off his clothes when he sees Edgar naked and pretending to be mad to elude capture. In this "gay" scene, Lear refers to Edgar as an "Athenian," an allusion to the Greek world in which male–male sexual love was common. The play remains within bounds in the character of Cordelia, the perfect heterosexual wife according to the dominant cultural script of the time, but in the characters of Goneril and Regan, the two bad sisters who betray and torment their father and drive him mad, the play takes serious issue with the dominant picture of male–female heterosexual relations. Both sisters are far indeed from the Elizabethan cultural ideal of a wife who is chaste, silent, and obedient. Each dominates her husband; both are adulterous with Edmund, Edgar's treacherous brother; and neither is especially obedient to their patriarchal father. They are referred to as monsters in the play, and it is their behavior that inspires the incredibly misogynist descriptions of women's bodies: "Down from the waist they're Centaurs / Though women all above: / But to the girdle do the gods inherit; / Beneath is all the fiend's: there's hell, there's darkness / There is the sulphurous pit – burning, scalding / Stench, consumption." This not altogether rosy picture of female genitalia might be said to occur at a point of conflict in Elizabethan culture between a dominant heterosexual cultural paradigm that would mandate the same gender roles for everyone and the reality of biological diversity. The anger evident in this passage would seem to register the feelings of someone who is ordered to have sex with women (under penalty of death, since "sodomy" or gay sex could result in execution) while experiencing desires at odds with the mandate. The play thus evokes gay experience and teasingly insinuates in the naked scene between Edgar and Lear that male love has value. Shakespeare is obliged to do this within the reigning gender paradigm, but that does not prevent him from mocking its assumptions, especially in the character of the all-licensing Clown, who at one point evokes the possibility that Goneril might force Lear into anal sex. This is no ordinary woman by any means.

The Scarlet Letter lends itself to a variety of Feminist and gender readings. First, it is a classic text regarding the representation of women. Hester is idealized as someone with specifically "feminine" talents such as sewing and caring for others. Women in the 19th century in America were educated to believe that their goal in life was to marry and to care for a family. The professions were off limits, and few women aspired to a life beyond the domestic sphere. By praising "feminine" talents such as sewing in Hester, Hawthorne pays her an ambivalent compliment, one that seems positive but that, from the perspective of women's rights and powers, has a negative undertow. It suggests women's proper sphere is the home in a role of caregiver to husband and children.

In addition, Hawthorne describes Hester as longing for engagement with the world of ideas around her. In an anachronism, those ideas would have been the democratic ideas that were animating popular uprisings against

monarchies in Europe around the time of the writing of the novel in 1849.
The uprisings of 1848 across Europe and Latin America sought to reform
reactionary governments and to make them more democratic. Female
friends of Hawthorne such as Margaret Fuller were involved in them. But
he disapproved and felt instead that women's natural identity and role in
life precluded such activities.

The novel also indirectly describes a historical shift that was occurring
by the mid-19th century in traditional patriarchal gender roles. At that
time, women were prevented from entering the professions largely by being
excluded from appropriate schooling. The justification for such exclusion
was that women's "sphere" was in the home because women were innately
endowed with a more caring disposition appropriate to child-rearing and
tending a household for a man whose own disposition was more geared
toward public endeavors and work. Men were strong, women weak; men
were competitive, aggressive, and domineering, women passive, gentle, and
submissive. In Hawthorne's novel, Hester Prynne is anything but submissive. When we meet her at the outset she is being released from prison,
and she has learned nothing from imprisonment. She is still defiant, and
her defiant spirit registers in the ornate design she has given the red A
for "adultery" that she is obliged to wear. Rather than say "I am sinful," the
letter advertises her great natural talent and skill. It is an emblem of beauty
rather than of sinfulness, guilt, and shame. Hester manifests strength in
many ways. She devotes herself to a singular, self-propelled path to
redemption by helping others. When her lover, Arthur, falters, she urges
him to be strong and to rebel against the Puritan authorities. Arthur is not
a typical male in the patriarchal paradigm. His sense of guilt makes him
weak. His gifts are intellectual rather than commercial. He falters and
lacks strength. But, with Hester's urging, he finally does rebel against the
oppressive moral system that ruins his life. Hawthorne depicts gender in
the process of transformation. Old models were giving way to new as
women laid claim to greater powers and rights. In part, the novel is a
meditation on the consequences of such a change.

Gender Theory would go further with the text. It would ask why it is so
important to Hawthorne that Hester should appear to have natural female
talents that suit her for domestic labor in life. The opening chapter, entitled
"The Custom House," is famous for being a summary of the themes of the
novel. One of the themes is masculinity. Hawthorne recounts how working
for the government had weakened him and made him less of a man. To
work for the government was a negative state of being for a Democrat of

that era, since Democrats preferred an ideal of male independence in economic life. Whigs were associated with the dependent life of government support and service. Democrats favored the idea that men were self-reliant and independent; they worked for themselves, not others. That political economic ideal is also an ideal of manly behavior. Men who are dependent on government or on others for sustenance are less manly according to this political gender ideology. Hawthorne finds that writing the novel is his way to re-find his lost masculinity because it allows him to practice a natural talent of his own. He can rely on his own abilities rather than rely on an institution like the government for support.

Dimmesdale's trajectory in the novel mirrors that of the author. Initially, he is in the thrall of other men who have more power than he has in society. He has given expression to his natural yearnings, but the institutions around him forbid such free expression, and so he feels guilt and lives a secretive life of self-hatred. Finally, with Hester's help, he throws off the oppressive influence of the state and church, under which he lives, and takes full responsibility for his nature. He confesses to the sin of adultery and acknowledges his natural family with Hester and Pearl. Although he dies, he achieves masculinity; he manifests strength and responsibility. Moreover, just before this final moment in the text, he gives a sermon which is characterized as a manifestation of an almost divine natural talent. Like Hawthorne in "The Custom House," he learns to speak for himself and to be self-reliant.

Queer Theorists would point out that this ideal of masculine achievement and renewal is based on a model of identity that is hierarchical. To be self-reliant, to manifest natural talent and manly independence, is to have clear, firm boundaries around oneself that demarcate the self-reliant self from supposedly external influences and dependencies. Yet it is the dependence on Hester that allows Dimmesdale to free himself from the oppressive influence of the Puritan church and state. Identity is not non-relational; it is always dependent and contingent. Moreover, it is hierarchical. To be what it wishes to be, the ideal of masculine identity in the novel must simultaneously posit a supportive female identity that sustains the male one and that is itself not capable of the same public achievement. Female identity is domestic identity, a balance to male public prerogatives. Even as it asserts a manly, self-reliant independence as its ideal to be imitated in the performance of daily gender identity, the masculine identity of Hawthorne and of Dimmesdale must simultaneously indicate that it is not natural at all and that it in fact is produced by a relation between contingent terms.

In addition, it is produced by what would appear to be homosexual panic. Dimmesdale, during his most "feminine" moments of dependence in the novel, lives with another man, Roger Chillingworth, who is described as probing his soul. He even at one point unfolds Dimmesdale's clothes while he sleeps to peer upon his naked body. Dimmesdale's attempt to achieve masculinity in the form of a renewal of his relationship with Hester is doubled by a parallel movement away from his intensely intimate relationship with Chillingworth. Fear of homosociality (if not of homosexuality) is at work in the formation of masculinity in the novel.

Citizen Kane is shaped by similar gender issues. Kane begins in a homosocial group made up of Bernstein, Leland, and himself. He is especially paired with Leland, and significantly, that friendship is broken by the arrival of Susan Alexander, whose opera-singing career Leland refuses to support by writing falsely praising reviews of singing he finds unprofessional. He is fired by Kane. Kane's entire life is shaped by a desire to fill in an absence created by his abandonment by his mother. His manic urge to achieve social power and to collect heaps of useless art treasures is suggestive of a compulsive need to fill in a breach in his being left by the withdrawal of a mother's affection while a child. That abandonment makes Kane seek to counter it by securing a mate like Susan who is much younger so that he can have power over her. Finally he can control the lost mother and make her give him the affection he feels he deserves. His sense of omnipotence and self-importance is linked to this need and this yearning. He compensates through public efforts at self-inflation for his sense of being someone who does not deserve a mother's affection. It is of note that he is on his way to a warehouse containing goods from his mother's home when he runs into Susan. She is a stand-in or substitute for the lost mother, and he displaces onto her his desire for his mother. In an interesting image, as she leaves him, a doll is placed in the lower left-hand corner of the frame to serve as a metaphor for his relationship to him. She is someone he seeks to control in order to restore a lost maternal presence. The glass container of floating snow is a similar metaphor; it suggests a well-contained identity, something easily controlled.

Citizen Kane also allows one to compare popular conceptions of gender with more critical ones. The poster for the film portrays Charles Foster Kane as a manly man who towers above others. But the purpose of the film is to question such stereotypes. Kane is portrayed as a man with emotional vulnerabilities. He lost his mother when he was young, and his life is driven by a longing to fill that breach. He idealizes women, only to discover they do

Figure 11   *Citizen Kane*. Produced and directed by Orson Welles. 1941.

not live up to the ideal. He attaches himself to a young woman he seeks to control fully, as if she were a puppet, in an attempt to control the anxiety-provoking situation of loss in his early childhood. He is a man with needs and yearnings for attachment to others, a far cry from the image of the resilient, tough figure who towers over women in the movie poster.

In a Queer reading, *Citizen Kane* would be characterized as a text about the instability and indeterminacy of gender. Kane's mother is such a source of trouble for his gender identity because she suffers herself from gender trouble. She is very masculine, and his father, comparatively, is very feminine (to use those categories as they are used in public discourse to indicate either strength and independence or weakness and dependence). His mother is cold and seems quite heartless. But she is only protecting Kane from the violence of her drunken husband, who physically abuses the boy. Nevertheless, she is depicted as possessing power in the family. She inherits the mines that make Kane a rich man, and she decides what is to be done with him (sending him east to be cared for by Thatcher, the banker) without consulting her husband, something that would have been considered the norm in a patriarchal society. At the outset, therefore, gender is depicted as unstable in the film. Actual gender practice seems to depart

Figure 12　Alamy B86112.

from the supposed natural norm. Later in the film, Kane will himself be "feminized" by his wife, when she discovers his tryst with Susan Alexander. She is portrayed as looming over him in the visual frame as she lectures him about how limited his options are in the situation. His absence of

Figure 13 *Citizen Kane*. Produced and directed by Orson Welles. 1941.

independence is portrayed as a dependent visual and social relationship to her. It is a movie in which women can be men and men women.

One of the more compelling meditations on gender identity in poetry is Elizabeth Bishop's poem "In the Waiting Room" (http://www.poemhunter.com/poem/in-the-waiting-room/). Before reading on, read the poem online, paying attention to moments where gender identity is evoked.

This is about as queer a poem as one might encounter. Bishop was a lesbian, and one way of reading the poem is to see it as the early perceptions by a lesbian girl of the gendered world around her. Like many poems, it is highly metaphorical. That is, ideas and feelings are expressed or described indirectly, and they are embodied in objects. The girl describes looking at a *National Geographic* magazine in the waiting room, while her aunt sees the dentist. The images of naked African women arouse her, and her sexual arousal is embodied in the concrete image or metaphor of a volcano. She is puzzled that she feels desire at the sight of naked women's bodies, but that would be expected of a lesbian girl. She is young enough still to think she is destined to be like the other heterosexual adults around her, so she does not yet realize she is different. She is still "in the waiting room" and is not an adult yet. Nevertheless, other metaphors embody her growing awareness of her difference, her own distinct gender identity. "Osa and

Martin Johnson / dressed in riding breeches" describes two European explorers who are indistinguishable by gender. The woman is dressed like a man. This evocation of a manly woman is followed by negative images of heterosexual or feminine women's lives: a dead man on a pole referred to as a "Long Pig," deformed babies, and women whose entrapment in marriage and child-rearing is registered in necks wound "round and round" with wire. They appear trapped, and they look like very undignified "light bulbs." The girl's incipient desire for other women appears as her reaction to the women's "horrifying" breasts which she is "too shy" to pause over. Her experience causes vertigo, and the vertigo has to do with her identity. She mistakes herself for her aunt, who is a "foolish, timid woman," an identity the young Elizabeth clearly does not admire. Then, she distinguishes herself as "an Elizabeth," but immediately wonders if she is "one of them," one of the heterosexual adults around her. She wonders about her heterosexual destiny and her feeling of difference: "Why should I be my aunt / or me, or anyone?" She notes that "those awful hanging breasts / held us all together," but she has also come to realize that she does not really feel an identification with "them," the timid, foolish women around her. She might be "like" them physically, but that she might be one of them seems to her "unlikely."

Her first perception is of her aunt, who seems a typically feminized heterosexual woman of the period. She is "timid," and she lets men (a male dentist) inflict what the child perceives as pain on her by poking around in her bodily cavities. The dentist's office might be considered a metaphor for compulsory heterosexuality. The child identifies with her aunt and feels her aunt's cry of pain in her own mouth, but she also disidentifies with her and feels her difference from her. She asks how she can be one of "them," meaning, perhaps all the gendered heterosexuals in the waiting room. She begins to experience both awakened desire toward women's bodies and repulsion from the female task of child-rearing. The metaphor for desire is the overflowing volcano. This sense of difference moves the child to ask why the expectation exists that all are "one." That, she says, seems "unlikely," since she of course does not at all feel like the other women in the room, given the awakened lesbian desire she feels looking at the naked women in the magazine. But the poem is not simply an expression of a lesbian awakening. Associated with lesbianism is the recognition that gender is easily confused, that men can be women, and women men. Posed against this insight into the indeterminacy and contingency of gender identity is a sense that compulsory heterosexuality keeps the free flow of transgender desire in check by restrictive means. Child-rearing is one method of control over women, and that is imaged as the winding of wire around women's necks: "naked women with necks / wound round and round with wire."

If one's biology can be so at odds with the mandates of patriarchal culture, mandates that say men have to be tough, aggressive, and independent and women weak, passive, and dependent, then it should not be surprising that culture is populated with stories about people who suffer from gender anxiety, a feeling that they somehow do not match the prevailing cultural ideal. If such anxiety is to be found in the life experience of a young lesbian girl, it probably also will be found in the experience of a heterosexual man who is not tough or aggressive or independent. Such is the case with *Fight Club*, a film that juxtaposes a passive and dependent male with an imaginary male he fantasizes himself being who fits more into the reigning patriarchal model for men. If the nameless main character succumbs to influence by Ikea and behaves like a quintessentially feminine woman in the patriarchal gender paradigm, fussing over internal decoration, the imaginary Tyler is an outgoing, aggressive, tough, violent, entrepreneurial male individualist. He wears leather, frequents dive bars, practices hard sex, and loves violence. He pushes the limit on tolerable behavior and pushes back against a world in which the main character passively acquiesces. If the main character allows himself to be hugged by the maternal, feminine Bob, Tyler turns Bob into a hardened soldier of the violent, all-male cause that is *Fight Club*. If Marla dominates Jack and ruins his various therapy experiences (which, with the Ikea shopping experience, are metaphors for how men are feminized in modern culture), Tyler turns her into his sex slave and manfully masters her. She and he enact a traditional sex gender paradigm that Jack can only fantasize about. The film indicts modern liberal culture for turning men into women and depriving them of their supposedly innate strength and masculinity. It offers an image of restoration to a prior "nature" in which men were more assertive and violent.

Fight Club is a good example of what gender critics calls "homosociality." That term is used for what we in the past might have referred to as "male bonding." The point is that all of our relationships are characterized by strong feelings of affection or "bonding" that resemble love relationships, be they straight or gay. This argument is made in order to undermine the justification for declaring homosexuality to be so different from heterosexuality that homosexuals merit different treatment. In order for men to adapt themselves to the patriarchal model for male behavior, they must identify with it, and usually this means they must identify with their father or with other male figures who embody patriarchal ideals such as strength, aggression, and independence. But to "identify with" is in some ways to love. At the core of heterosexuality is always a homosexual moment of "bonding" when a new inductee is initiated into the culture of patriarchy. In primitive cultures, this moment was ritualized. Boys left with their fathers on a journey, or separated themselves with older men from women for a period. *Fight Club* has such a moment when the main character identifies with Tyler (his missing father) and separates himself from the modern, liberal, feminized world in which he had lived previously and makes a home in a derelict building. His relationship with Tyler is homosocial. It consists of one man's love for another. Its purpose is to "rescue" the main character from feminization and to turn him into a properly heterosexual male within the patriarchal way of defining such terms. But for that to occur male–male love must do its work of separating the young man from excessive dependence on maternal influences in his life. *Fight Club* thus shows us the most primitive structures of gender formation in modern culture, but it also reveals the trouble within the reigning gender categories that leads to gender identity anxiety in the first place. Biologically, the main character is what he is – a nice guy who is not an overly tough, aggressive "man." That such forms of masculine identity are intolerable to some and the source of great anxiety to others is interesting because it suggests that biology is at odds with patriarchy. Patriarchy is not the nature that one regains by putting modern feminine culture aside. It has to be manufactured, because nature does not match its ideal models for men.

Things to Look for in Literary and Cultural Texts

- How are women and men depicted? What era is the text produced in and how might that make a difference in how the two genders are portrayed?

- How are gender relations constructed in the work? Are they equal or unequal? Is one gender privileged over another? If so, how and for what reasons?

- Is gender stable or unstable in the work? Can the text be queered by showing how its gender constructs are indeterminate or contingent?

8

Ethnic, Post-Colonial, and Transnational Criticism

Major Texts

W. E. B. Du Bois, *The Souls of Black Folks*
Franz Fanon, *The Wretched of the Earth*
Edward Said, *Orientalism*
G. C. Spivak, "Three Women's Texts and a Critique of Imperialism"
Homi Bhabha, *Nation and Narration*
Mike Hill, *Whiteness: A Critical Reader*
Rey Chow, *Writing Diaspora*
David Palumbo-Liu, *Streams of Cultural Capital*

Major Ideas

- Human culture is divided along ethnic and national lines. Wherever and however humans band together – for reasons of consanguinity or ethnicity or for reasons of tribal or political organization – they constitute unique and different cultures.

- Humans' tendency to identify themselves in terms of ethnicity, nationality, or geography means that human culture frequently is expressive of the concerns of highly specific groups of people. For example, the musical and song form called the "blues" arose in the context of the enslavement of a sizeable African population by European-descended Whites in the Americas over a period of three and a half centuries.

An Introduction to Criticism: Literature / Film / Culture, First Edition. Michael Ryan.
© 2012 Michael Ryan. Published 2012 by Blackwell Publishing Ltd.

- Colonialism consisted of the forced occupation of entire nations by other nations who exploited the colonized country economically. Modern colonialism lasted until the late 20th century. Post-Colonial Studies examines cultures of colonialism as well as the vexed cultural situation that arose after colonialism ended.

- An ethnic group that is dominant often, either deliberately or unconsciously, makes its group's traits normative in that society. For example, Whites in the United States from the 19th century on operated with the often explicit assumption that Whiteness was a norm that equated with greater intelligence, civility, and morality.

- Globalization, the spread internationally of capitalist markets and the growing interconnectedness of national economies, has fostered a new transnational culture characterized by shared literary and popular cultural forms and flows across national borders of cultural creativity.

Major Terms

Ethnicity/Race   Now that humans' genetic make-up is available for study, it has become clear that *Homo sapiens* divides into five rough regionally defined racial groupings. Africans and Asians look different and are genetically different. How significant those differences are and what they consist of remains to be determined. In recent years, scholars of culture have argued that race is a cultural fabrication that often serves crude power interests (justifying slavery and colonization, for example). Racialist thinking does have that function, but race is only in part culturally or socially constructed. Most of our negative beliefs about other ethnic groups are cultural fabrications that express feelings like fear, envy, resentment, and hatred, but the five major racial groups of humanity are nevertheless real things.

Diaspora   The condition of ethnic homelessness whereby a group that once had a homeland is deprived of it or is obliged for economic reasons to emigrate elsewhere and to live abroad.

Cultural Appropriation   The borrowing or use of the forms of one culture by another, usually a culture that is in a more dominant position. For example, Black rhythm and blues was appropriated by Whites in rock and roll.

Orientalism   Both the attitude and the body of knowledge that fostered and supported the colonization of the "Orient," from the Middle East to China. Such knowledge worked by stereotyping the "Orient," erasing the detail of life there, and turning the East into a simple, easily grasped category that was understandable within the Western scheme of knowledge.

Nationalism/Transnationalism   Nationalism is the belief in the superiority of one's own nation. Nationalists adopt a defensive posture toward other cultures, peoples, and nations, and they resist cultural mixing through migratory flows of people across borders. Transnationalism refers to the contemporary cultural world of relations, influences, intersections, and hybridizations across national borders and cultural boundaries.

Subaltern   The condition of the colonized. It implies subordination to the power and will of the colonizer.

Cultural Imperialism   The dominance of one nation's culture over the culture of other nations. Hollywood movies are often cited as an example. Much better funded than local national movie industries, Hollywood can easily dominate the market, and such dominance means that local national production cannot survive without government protection.

Third World   An older term for economically underdeveloped countries in the late 20th century.

Summary and Discussion

Ethnic differences are a curious fact of human life. They seem to account for minor variations within humanity, many if not most of which seem to have to do with inconsequential external features such as eye shape or skin color. But differences between ethnic groups can also be quite noticeable and remarkable. What counts as good singing in South Asia is different from what counts as good in English choral singing, for example. In literature, the differences are less marked. A novel by Salman Rushdie is not that different from a novel by his fellow magic realist Gabriel García Márquez, but it is quite distinct in form and content from the works of Alice Munro, a Canadian female short story writer. Cultural difference between South Asia and Anglo-America become more marked if one compares film styles. Bollywood, with its routine musical interludes and magnified melodramatic motifs, noticeably differs from the standards of Hollywood. That cultural differences are usually geographic is itself suggestive of their possible physical roots.

Native American literature, which initially was oral but which has in recent decades emerged into print form in English, can be said to be different in sensibility to the literature of the mostly European- and African-descended writers of contemporary North America. In novels such as Leslie Marmon Silko's *Ceremony*, for example, or in Louise Erdrich's *Love Medicine*, the traditional linear narrative form that characterizes most fiction is replaced by circular forms that are reflective of Indian religious and mythological assumptions about the circular character of nature. Moreover, the stories emphasize yearnings to return home, unlike most narratives, which usually have to do with a departure from home. Indian stories also are reflective of the Indian experience of trauma at the hands of Europeans during the era of conquest and colonization. The stories are usually fragmentary and multiple, and they are about lives that have been displaced from a single linear development toward self-fulfillment by the traumas of disinheritance. Deprived of property by conquest and left out of an economic world monopolized by other ethnic groups, Indian culture has no secure past that can be the basis for a secure narrative move into the future.

While some Indian writers pursue a vision of Indian authenticity and are nostalgic for a lost Indian identity associated with oral story-telling and mythologies that emphasize the circularity of nature and of history, others emphasize more dissonant aspects of Indian culture. Rather than call for respect for traditional beliefs or for the sacred embodied in Indian myths, these stories emphasize the trickster tales and the new reality of mixed-blood identity in Indian life. The trickster is a common figure in Indian myths, who breaks rules, overturns hierarchies, and plays tricks on others. Gerald Vizenor draws on the pervasive stories of tricksters who upset settled norms and institutions for the sake of creative play to satirize the nativist concept of Indian identity. Trickster writing nevertheless affirms a distinct form that is peculiar to Indian culture even as the trickster form claims to be "postindian." Louis Owens argues that the metaphor of the mixed-blood Indian is representative of a new age of cultural and genetic mixing that has replaced the old single-identity tradition of Indian culture, an identity that is rendered complex by the reality of multiple tribes, from Choctaw to Ojibwa. An argument could be made that in fact there never was a single "Indian" literature or culture.

In the American literary tradition, African American literature makes a special case of its own for the notion of ethnic uniqueness, be that the effect of biology or the result of history. Enslavement bred experiences that no other ethnic group had to undergo in America, and the resulting literary works, from the autobiography of Frederick Douglass to the anti-Jim Crow stories of Richard Wright, map a distinct emotional landscape and a highly specific set of life events, from being chased by a lynch mob to having to fight a white overseer who literally "owns" one in order to attain the same freedom that most enjoy simply by virtue of being born. The experience of subjugation fostered a range of reactions in African Americans, from rage and revolt to acquiescence and assimilation. The 18th-century poetry of Phyllis Wheatley is an example of the latter approach. Wheatley occasionally referred to her status as a Black in an America dominated by Whites, but for the most part her poetry explores Christian and neoclassical themes of the kind that were common in poetry by Whites at the time: "Twas mercy brought me from my Pagan land, / Taught my benighted soul to understand / That there's a God, that there's a Saviour too: / Once I redemption neither sought nor knew. / Some view our sable race with scornful eye, / 'Their colour is a diabolic dye.' / Remember, Christians, Negroes, black as Cain, / May be refin'd, and join th' angelic train." If Wheatley's argument essentially is that white sugar can be made from brown, other Black writers adopted an angrier, separatist approach to the experience of slavery. David Walker's "Appeal" on behalf of the "colored people of the world" goes so far as to argue in favor of armed rebellion of a kind that did indeed occur during and after the time in which he wrote early in the 19th century. He contended that America belonged to those whose actual labor had built it: "Let no man of us budge one step, and let slave-holders come to beat us from our country. America is more our country, than it is the whites – we have enriched it with our blood and tears."

African American writing was shaped by the experience of slavery for many years after its legal abolition. It was in a way a case of ethnic trauma, an event so negative and so powerful that it affected the lives of African Americans through many generations. It represented the disinheriting of Blacks, the taking away of the accumulated property that accrued to all other ethnic groups over time and that was passed on from one generation to the next, so that each generation could do better than the one before. For Blacks that process was made impossible or was delayed for a long time by slavery, which was essentially a theft of property on a large scale. Moreover, the attitudes bred by slavery gave rise to a lingering racism against Blacks, which took the form of excluding them from access to economic life and to wealth and was a further iteration of disinheritance. The physical violation that was the slave experience continued as lynching for those who dared to revolt or to stand above the subjugated mass. In the years following World War I, for example, over a hundred Blacks a year were lynched by Whites. Only in the 1960s, a full century after the Civil War whose ostensible purpose was to end slavery, did Blacks finally begin to achieve a measure of civil equality with Whites. And even though many Blacks in the decades that followed entered the ranks of the professions and the political elite, many others, largely due to the legacy of disinheritance, continue to live in poverty to a much greater degree than Whites.

The pressure of the White norm on Blacks in America is felt in the work of Charles Chesnutt and Nella Larsen. Larsen's *Passing* is the story of a woman of African American and Anglo-American heritage who can "pass" for White and does so until she is exposed. The irony of the practice of passing is that Whites cannot really tell the difference between themselves and other races unless it is drawn to their attention. And if racial difference has to be pointed out, is it really significant? Chesnutt's *The Marrow of Tradition* is concerned with a different kind of passing, that of professional Blacks who fit into White professional society to a certain degree but who in times of crisis are obliged to choose between the dominant White culture and their own Black culture. Chesnutt's novel explores the irony of a culture in which White racists who feel Blacks are inferior and deserve mistreatment discover that the lives of their loved ones depend on the skills of a Black doctor.

Such works undermine the premises of White racism and they point forward toward a world in which racial categories cease to be relevant measures or standards. Nevertheless, race is real both in a social sense and in a cultural sense. In times of economic recession, Blacks are less likely to get jobs than Whites when they are equally or even better qualified. The powerful natural drive to protect one's own means that "others" must be excluded whenever possible from resources that may benefit one's own racial kin, those in relation to whom one's own identity is formed. But decades of disinheritance also foster the impression that Blacks have not only been disinherited but deserve to be disinherited. White literature often has abetted that assumption. One of the most racist writers in the American tradition, William Faulkner, believed that Whites and Blacks were like cats and dogs; to expect them to mate and mix would be unnatural. His novel *Light in August* concerns a mixed-race man named Joe Christmas, who murders a white woman and is then shot and castrated by a lynch mob. Nothing in the novel leads one to think the punishment was unjust or inappropriate. On the contrary, Joe is associated negatively with the kind of woman proud, pro-slavery Southerners like Faulkner were inclined to hate: representatives of the Northern liberal pro-abolitionist group that sought the South's defeat in the Civil War to make Blacks equal with Whites. Joe murders Miss Burden when she offers to fund a college education for him so that he can advance himself in the world. Juxtaposed to the fallen world of racial mixture and misguided attempts to rectify nature through state intervention stands the ideal of a world outside history, a place of spirit and universal truth that is timeless. This is the world of the Confederate pro-slavery cavalry which forever rides in the memory of Reverend Hightower, a man who does without the women who are associated with the breaching of natural boundaries and the breaking of moral rules and who are the occasion for all that is bad in Faulkner's moral universe in the novel. Women such as Lena Grove are determined to be good mothers, and they carry a strong moral center, organized around the patriarchal ideal of fatherhood, within them. Her quest to return to Jefferson, named after the US president who gave the states' rights ideology that supported slavery its most potent justification and whose version of anti-governmental democracy fueled the defense of slavery against Northern statist attempts at reform, is at the same time a quest to re-find the proper father of her child and to re-establish a norm of White child-breeding that would offset the dangerous racial mixing that is at the root of evil in the novel. The violent removal of Joe's genitals thus coincides in the plot with the birth of a pure White child who bears the promise of a restored Whiteocracy in the South, something that, like the memory of the Confederate cavalry ever riding in Reverend Hightower's mind, has something sacred and timeless about it.

Faulkner's complex "modernist" style is often held up as a justification for ignoring the racist arguments of his works. That style emphasizes the confused and complex character of the world; it is a place where good motives go astray, good people are abused easily by bad, and formal ideals of moral virtue are often at odds with natural virtue. These are standard "democratic" arguments bequeathed by Jeffersonian and Jacksonian democracy from the 19th century, and they draw on the same anti-government naturalism that flows into Southern racism in the American 20th century and makes it resistant to state pressure to reform itself. God-in-nature is a more powerful standard than any artificial norm the government, especially the Northern pro-abolition government, might seek to impose, from the Civil War through the New Deal of the 1930s, when Faulkner wrote. The complex modernism of the style is a way of emphasizing the fallen character of the world, the fact that it is beyond remediation or repair. One should turn instead to the realm of timeless spirituality, where the Confederate cavalry rides forever, bravely trying to save the natural superiority of Whites over Blacks and stave off the danger of anti-natural racial mixture. Faulkner was of the same world as the Southern New Critics, the American Formalist critics who believed that literature embodied spirit in a paradoxical unity of form and content, and it should not be surprising that his work emphasizes the same sense that the world is paradoxical and immune to secular reason of the kind that animates liberal efforts to use government to reform social ills such as racism.

With time, such conservative arguments have lost ground and been displaced by anti-racist liberalism. Liberals labor to eliminate racism by advocating greater tolerance and generosity. In a film like *2012*, they argue that the human community must outgrow the natural conservatism that dictates that we should save our own before caring for others, and they populate the list of primary characters with Black actors in a surprising and innovative move that makes real the ideal they are promoting.

Racial difference was often the justification for colonialism during its modern incarnation from the Renaissance to the present. The Irish were thought to be a lesser race by the English, as were the inhabitants of South Asia. Differences in levels of economic, social, and technological development assisted the legitimation of the seizure of others' land and resources by making it appear as if Europeans were a superior race. The alacrity with which formerly "lesser" people have caught up technologically, economically, and socially undermines the racist assumption, but for several centuries it served the interests of those willing to put aside scruples for rubles. It is one of the ironies of history that the very evolutionary theories used in the late 19th century by racists to justify the violence and rapacity of colonialism probably provided a better explanation of their activities than of those of their victims. Inferiority in a genetic sense may consist of too strong an assertion, primate-style, of one's own sense of one's own superiority. Dominance behavior looks as stupid in humans as it does in apes.

Many scholars of literature and culture attend to the relations between colonial powers and their colonies, while others look at the legacies of colonialism around the world. Edward Said launched Post-Colonial Studies by arguing that the West's "orientalist" knowledge of the colonized was largely stereotypical. The colonial experience appears obliquely in many examples of British literature, from the way contact with Indian religion influences the rise of the spiritualism of the Romantic movement, especially in the work of William Wordsworth, to the description of cross-cultural misunderstanding in Forster's *Passage to India*. In some works of literature, the colonies serve as a metaphor for the repressed "other" side of civility – the urges and desires we repress in order to live together in civilized societies. In Charlotte Brontë's *Jane Eyre*, Mrs. Rochester, the mentally handicapped wife of the man Jane falls in love with and ultimately marries, is a woman of color from the colonies who figures as the wild other against whose madness the novel's ideal of White bourgeois civility is defined. All that is perverse about English "normality" is projected onto the "madwoman in the attic." The colonies thus served a number of figurative or thematic purposes in British literature. They were the ideal of an alternative reality, but they were also the hidden underside of civilized life, the place where all that the English feared and detested in themselves could take up residence in sort of figurative and psychological internal exile.

In the American tradition, colonization largely focused on Native Americans. The difference between the conservative and liberal sides of American culture manifested themselves in the difference between William Bradford's celebration of the massacre of the Pequots as a "sweet sacrifice" that did a conservative God's will and the more liberal Roger Williams, who made friends of the Indians in Rhode Island and wrote a dictionary of their language. Democrats such as William Fenimore Cooper tended to romanticize the Native population in novels such as *The Last of the Mohicans*, and eventually the romantic elegies and eulogies ended up having a predictive effect. The Natives did not last long. John Tanner's remarkable *The Falcon*, an account of a White boy's life after abduction by Natives whose world he joins, depicts a Native culture that was easily and readily succumbing to the lure of the colonists.

Mainstream European American fiction of the era such as Hawthorne's *Scarlet Letter* uses the Natives as symbolic markers. When Hester points westward toward freedom from Whig moral government, she is making a familiar Democratic Party gesture toward western settlement as a means of redistributing property and providing economic opportunity to poor people. But she is also pointing toward Indian lands that the Democratic Party was claiming (and stealing) for its constituents. Natives in the novel are associated with Roger Chillingworth, the most negative moral character.

One consequence of colonialism is the transformation wrought by the experience of immigration. Franz Fanon examined the experience of having to wear "white masks" to get by in Europe, of having to bend one's own identity so as to appear to the colonizer to be free of all taint of primitive "native" traits. Colonial interaction also served to spur a sense of pride in one's own culture and a drive to explore its specific themes and forms. "Negritude" was the name for one such movement in African literature in response to French colonialism.

Examples of Post-Colonial and Ethnic Analysis

Joseph Conrad's *Heart of Darkness*, which is frequently misread as a critique of colonialism, is a remarkably racist statement of the pro-colonialist position at the time. The novel does criticize a certain kind of colonialism – the soft-hearted, unmanly, liberal-reformist variety that would bring "civilization" to African Blacks – but it condones a much harsher, more supposedly "realistic" treatment of Black Africans. Conrad's conservative position is that all civilization is a sham because it covers over and fatuously wishes away the disposition toward violence inherent in human nature. Conservatives like Conrad believe humans are depraved and therefore need to be controlled by strong leaders who impose an authoritarian order on an otherwise unruly society. Liberals are to blame for the worst aspects of colonialism because they mistakenly believe humans can be improved and made good. That belief, according to Conrad, is especially misguided in Africa, the "heart of darkness," with darkness being understood here both geographically and ethnographically. It is the dark heart conservatives see in all humanity, the thing that makes liberal hopes to improve the world fatuous and silly.

Marlowe, the narrator, takes a job with the Belgian company in charge of the ivory-producing colony of the Congo in Africa. He travels up the Congo River toward the camp of Kurtz, an ivory trader who has adopted native ways and increased ivory production. But his ways are violent and ruthless rather than benevolent and kind (the path chosen by the benevolent missionary society, which is represented as being lost and misguided, wandering aimlessly through the primeval forest). Marlowe discovers that Kurtz has gone over to the side of the Blacks, taken a Black woman as his wife, and come to embrace the truth of the "heart of darkness" that life is cruel and violent and that one must be cruel and violent to succeed. The racism of the novel resides in its assignment of a cruel and violent "nature" to Black Africans, when the truth of that period in history was that it was White Europeans who were behaving with enormous cruelty toward Africans, often cutting off the hands and feet of children who did not produce enough rubber for the Belgian colonial enterprise. At the heart of this conservative animosity toward ethnic others, those very different from themselves, is, the novel suggests, a fear of women. Kurtz's African wife is presented as threatening and powerful, and when asked what Kurtz's final words were by Kurtz's fiancée back in Europe, Marlowe says "your name," when in fact the words were "the horror, the horror." Woman is the "horror" because she represents principles of care and empathy within European culture that are threatening emblems of weakness (and thus of susceptibility to harm) to a conservative like Conrad. To confront the heart of darkness in this conservative conception of the world as a space of mutual predation, one must be tough and strong, and any taint of femininity means possible death. Woman is therefore the "horror" of potential weakness in men that leads to extermination in the brutal struggle to survive. Frequently, public attitudes such as racism and pro-colonialism are bound up with highly personal feelings, fantasies, and fears with genetic roots. In this case, the conservative disposition toward violence in human affairs justified by a conception of men as tough, aggressive, and dominant is probably fueled by a genetic mandate toward survival that required these traits in humans' ancestral past. Confronted by the liberal critique of colonialism in the late 19th century, Conrad, who was quite reactionary in his politics, responded with a story of how misguided such liberalism is. What is interesting is that his vision of nature is itself nature speaking through him. In conservatives like Conrad linger antique genetic programs that make it seem necessary for men to still fight like animals even though they have entered a period in history dominated by much greater levels of liberal civility.

The arrival in the home country of immigrants from the colonies, who were, as a result of colonialism, as much British "subjects" as any Anglo-Saxon, transformed the literature and culture of England. For example, Hanif Kureishi's screenplay for the movie *My Beautiful Laundrette* concerns a young Pakistani man who is given a laundromat to run by his uncle. He has an affair with a White punk named Johnny, and together they make the laundrette a success. Made at a time when England was characterized by strong conservative racist movements such as the National Front, the film also depicts racist violence against South Asians. Indeed, the plot at times hinges on either racist attacks on people of color or counter-attacks by them against White racists. The film is important because it exercises a displacement of perspective of a kind that is necessary if different ethnic groups are to inhabit the same social space without violence. Kureishi obliges the viewer, especially the White English viewer, to adopt the perspective of another ethnic group and to identify with the concerns of a different kind of "Englishman," one whose skin tone and ethnic affiliation would have merited him the derisive term "wog" just a generation back. To the degree that literature and film can be said to have useful social functions, they would in part be the displacement of perspectives that too readily lend themselves to attitudes and actions that undermine the ideal of civility by conducting human thought and behavior toward violence against feared and hated ethnic others. If conservative civilization in the past has consisted of the subordination of multiple perspectives to a single, mono-ethnic, economically and politically domi-nant perspective, modern liberal civility consists always of a balance of perspectives such that no single one is central or dominant. It requires tolerance for diversity of a kind that is fostered by the ability to imagine others' lives, concerns, and ways of seeing things.

With the rise to economic power of formerly colonized or partially colonized countries such as India, China, and Brazil, it is difficult to continue speaking of those parts of the world or of their cultures as being "post-colonial." Moreover, as modern media develop and as publishing and film production internationalize, new forms of transnational culture come into being. Indeed, "transnationality" may be a more relevant term in the contemporary era than "post-coloniality." It speaks to the new reality in which former colonies are no longer shadowed by their colonial legacy and in which non-Western centers of cultural production such as China or Japan become as influential as similar centers in the West, especially in regard to film production.

The critical analysis of literature and culture becomes difficult in a transnational context. Certain human concerns are indeed universal, but the way they play out is often inflected locally according to custom, mores, and national cultural style. And those are quite multiple. Most ideally demand a knowledge of the local language to be fully comprehended. But a new "international style" in writing and publishing makes it possible to overcome some of these localist barriers and difficulties. A new international language of references, allusions, and metaphors has developed along with an international culture based on shared or overlap-ping interests. Haruki Murakami is Japanese, but he really writes for an international audience. Luc Besson is French and Roland Emmerich is German, but their films, from *The Fifth Element* to *2012*, are international in theme and style. *Il Postino* (*The Postman*) is an Italian film about a famous South American writer living in exile in Italy. Kirin Dsai's novel

The Inheritance of Loss concerns an immigrant laborer in New York who decides to return home to India.

Murakami's novel *Sputnik Sweetheart* (*Supuutoniku no koibito*) is typical of the new cultural internationalism. Unlike other international works such as Jhumpa Lahiri's *The Namesake*, which gives narrative expression to a nostalgia for cultural roots in a world that celebrates the interchangeability of cultures, Murakami's novel explores the dangers and rewards of letting go of one's national origins and of experiencing the uprootedness of transnational existence in a globalized world context (if one has the money, that is, a reality astutely highlighted in the novel). The metaphor of the "Sputnik" (a Russian spacecraft of the 1950s that was launched with a dog on board that was never retrieved), which characterizes the human condition of loneliness, is itself an index of internationalism, a taking of meaning from events outside one's own national orbit. Murakami's cultural references, to everything from *La Bohème* to Jack Kerouac, place the novel in an international frame of reference, as they draw attention to the fact that the novel is intended for an educated cultural elite that can appreciate allusions to the hills of Tuscany and the islands of Greece while understanding what it means to be Korean in Japan or Japanese in Switzerland. The novel explores how vexed boundaries can be in a culture of enormous commonality across highly diverse populations. Heterosexual passion confronts homosexual exclusion and vice versa. Japanese meets internally excluded Korean. A Korean is bruised by the small town provincialism of Switzerland, even as the town celebrates a week of musical high culture that supposedly is international and inclusive. Even as it crosses boundaries with ease, the novel is about the danger of crossing boundaries. Balanced against tender affection is the possibility of anonymous predatory brutality.

Ethnic criticism is often concerned with the representation of ethnic minorities in the culture of the dominant ethnic group. Many American films, including *Citizen Kane*, concern White lives, and Blacks appear in the films often in only glancing references or asides. There is only one reference to Blacks in the film, and that occurs when Kane and Susan, his young wife, are fighting in his tent during one of his mammoth "picnics" along the California seashore, which more resemble caravans in the desert. The film cuts from an image of Kane striking Susan to an image of Black jazz musicians. It is as if wildness, loss of control, and descent into the jungle of human violence is being coded as Black. That was not the intent of the filmmakers. Welles was famous for siding with non-Whites and the poor; his efforts in that regard pretty much cost him his Hollywood career.

Figure 14   *Citizen Kane.* Produced and directed by Orson Welles. 1941.

But culture contains stereotypes that even the most enlightened draw on, and sometimes those stereotypes are laced with old and forgotten racialist assumptions.

Things to Look for in Literary and Cultural Texts

- How does the work represent race or ethnicity? What meaning does race or ethnicity have in the work? It is a stigma or a source of pride and self-identity? Is it a way of questioning the authority of powerful social groups or a way of asserting that power? Is race used ideologically to justify one group's power over another?

- Is one ethnic group's perspective or point of view given more prominence or value than that of another group? If so, what is the reason for this? Is the ethnic group in question in a position of power or dominance or is it subordinate and disempowered? How are relations between dominant and subordinate racial groups represented?

- Is race portrayed as a natural feature that justifies racialist attitudes? Or is it treated sociologically as a mechanism for branding and excluding people from resources and power?

- In works dealing with colonialism, how are the relations between colonizers and colonized depicted? Does the work justify or critique colonialism? How are home and nation related in the minds of post-colonial subjects living in conditions of diaspora?

- In international works, how are national cultures and the differences between cultures represented? How are characters in these works the same as or different from characters in other kinds of literature and culture? What is international about the imagery used or the themes explored? Does the work describe an international culture or international cultural imperialism?

9

Scientific Criticism

Major Texts

Charles Darwin, *The Origin of Species*
Brian Boyd, *On the Origin of Stories*
Joseph Carroll, *Literary Darwinism*
George Lakoff, *Metaphors We Live By*
Lisa Zunshine, *Strange Concepts and the Stories They Make Possible*
Ellen Spolsky, *Satisfying Skepticism*
Patrick Hogan, *Cognitive Science, Literature, and the Arts*
Harold Fromm, *The Ecocriticism Reader*

Major Ideas

- Scientific criticism ranges from the cognitive sciences to evolutionary studies to ecology or the study of natural environments. Cognitive literary studies are concerned with the operations of the mind both in regard to how literary works are constructed and in regard to how the mind of the reader engages with the literary work. Evolutionary Studies is concerned with the way humanity's genetic nature manifests itself in literature and culture. Ecocriticism examines the role of the environment in literature.

An Introduction to Criticism: Literature / Film / Culture, First Edition. Michael Ryan.
© 2012 Michael Ryan. Published 2012 by Blackwell Publishing Ltd.

- The telling of a story or the construction of a poem is a cognitive act. It is an operation of the mind. A work of literature will therefore reflect how the mind operates as it organizes experience. The reading or viewing of a work of literature is also a cognitive event. Readers or viewers bring to the engagement with the work mental schemas that allow them to organize the experience of reading or viewing. But reading or viewing also consists of allowing one's experience to be orchestrated and guided in certain ways. In the most obvious example of such orchestration, the detective story writer deliberately misleads the reader by limiting access to knowledge and by providing mistaken knowledge.

- All cultural events such as a work of literature or a film are also natural events. They are physical, and they have physical effects. Literature manifests the most fundamental imperatives of natural life inasmuch as life is the end result of a genetically motivated evolution over time. The themes of literature are understandable in terms of adaptations that have facilitated human evolution, and cultural works are functional within the framework of evolution. They further the well-being (the survival) of the human species by promulgating norms that diminish violence and further cooperative behavior, training humans to recognize dangers to survival, and provide models of thought and behavior suitable to life in cooperative environments that assist survival.

- Literary themes that embody evolution range from violence and war to love and marriage. The tendency toward violence in humans is a response to adverse environments (often populated by predators) that made a capacity for violence an adaptation that increased human fitness to survive and reproduce. Humans carry with them still those ancient ancestral adaptive dispositions. Humans also spend much of their lives courting, mating, and reproducing. Literature and culture is often concerned with these aspects of human behavior, and the issues and concerns that arise in these areas of life can be understood in evolutionary terms.

- Humans live in physical environments and interact with them in significant ways. To live as a human is to live physically in a particular place. The physical environment is not referred to in every work of literature or culture, yet it hovers in the background as an essential, if invisible, dimension of human life. It also often is an important measure of human success or an important test of human ability in human stories.

Major Terms

Natural Selection   The process whereby organisms survive in adverse environments through the random mutation of their genes from one generation to the next. Some mutations make survival possible and are retained in the organism through survival and successful reproduction.

Gene/Genetic   Genes regulate the life of organisms by passing on inherited traits.

Genotype   The genetic make-up of an organism that determines what it is and how it functions. It consists of the inherited instructions carried by a genetic code that determine what it is.

Phenotype   The particular way a genotype manifests itself in observable traits in organisms.

Fitness   An organism that survives in an adverse environment proves its fitness. That it is fit to survive can also be understood to mean that it fits with its environment. Random genetic mutations have resulted in this particular organism's ability to continue in existence and to reproduce despite the threats to survival the environment poses. Inclusive Fitness is a related term that means that humans strive to optimize the survival of close kin.

Adaptive/Adaptation   Genetic mutations are random, but some are retained through natural selection because they are adaptive. They assist the organism in surviving in an adverse environment that is fatal to similar organisms that did not benefit from the genetic mutation that is adaptive.

Epigenesis   The process whereby the same genes express themselves differently depending on the environment. A small leaf plant may generate broad leaves in response to a change in environment such as a drop in rainfall.

Gene Culture Coevolution   Humans have evolved culture as an adaptive ability to enable survival. Culture consists of stored information that is inherited, much as genes are inherited. Human-made cultural environments in turn affect genetic evolution.

Sociobiology   The study of species that considers the consequences for natural selection of certain forms of social behavior.

Reproductive Success   The passing on of genes from one generation to the next. The term also characterizes fitness. The more fit organisms achieve greater reproductive success than those that are not fit and do not survive in adverse environments.

Dominance   Animals attain status within groups, and those with high status are dominant. They often control access to females when they are male or control the distribution of resources when they are female.

Embodied Mind   The idea that cognition is influenced by the body in which it takes place. Our ideas and categories are projections of our bodily experiences.

Schema (also Image Schema)   An ordering device of the mind that allows us to process experience according to already held mental categories such as space and time.

Conceptual Metaphor   Human thought uses metaphors (transfers from one domain to another) to understand and describe the world. So, we discuss life in terms of war ("It was a real struggle, but I figured it out.")

Ecology   Ecology is the study of the interactions of organisms with their environments.

Summary and Discussion

Critics have begun to borrow from the sciences to understand literature and culture. Three important areas of inquiry are evolution, cognition, and the environment.

Cognitive psychology studies how the mind processes its experience of the world. One of the major operations of the mind, one that is central to literature, is the transfer of a perception or thought from one domain to another that is similar or analogous (that has the same proportion). "Analogy" means one thing has the same shape as another, and shape is a physical characteristic. One of the central ideas of cognitive psychology is that thought is physical. It follows patterns that are derived from our bodily experience of the world. Those include directionality and containment. We think about the world in terms of such bodily activities as movement and such bodily models as inside and outside (a container). Some basic cognitive schemas we use are path, balance, and contact – all things that pertain to our bodily experience of the world. These schemas allow us to organize our experience so that we can act in ways that are functional and appropriate to our life context. As I "plan the day ahead," I use several schemas – time (day), direction (ahead), and agency/action (plan). The basic schemas that organize experience are time and space, but there are many others, from attraction to equilibrium. Highly abstract theories in the social and physical sciences often display hidden metaphors rooted in physical life, such as "center/periphery" or "origin/derivation." According to cognitive psychology, this is true of all thought, no matter how logical or formal.

Evolutionary Studies also assumes humans are natural beings. We humans have survived on earth because we have adapted to changing environments. Those adaptations were generated by random genetic mutations that over time became permanent features of humanity because those bearing the mutations survived the hazards that their environment posed more readily than those who did not benefit from the mutation. Random mutations make accidentally for an ability to survive (adapt to an environmental danger), and that ability was passed on through human reproduction. Those with the new characteristic (such as an ability to outrun predators or to use new larger brains to communicate and cooperate) were more fit to survive in their environment. Adaptations generated by random genetic mutations have thus been functional in some way in human life. They have assisted survival and enabled those with the adaptation to reproduce.

In evolutionary theory, human culture is seen as playing an important role in maintaining the existence of the human species. About 30,000 years ago, humans began to form larger settled communities that became the first civilizations. Those communities required more advanced cognitive abilities, abilities that did not previously exist in the species. Some of those abilities made civilization possible, but others were the product of adaptations solicited by the new human-made environments. Such products of adaptations in human cognitive abilities as writing and laws and trade became essential requirements of human survival. Civilizations would not have been possible without them. The ability of humans to survive in communities where only some were responsible for food production while others looked after manufacture, trade, defense, and administration came to be dependent on culture, on the passing on of information from one generation to the next. Culture was an adaptation that facilitated the emergence of large cooperative communities founded on a division of labor. Central to culture was a mental ability we call imagination – the ability to picture things in one's mind with one's eyes closed. That kind of cognition is called "super-sensory" because it is not generated by objects in the world that one senses with eyes and ears. The thing or object is in the mind only. Writing is made possible by super-sensory cognition because we understand an invisible idea by looking at marks on a page. Similarly, laws are ideas of justice embodied in institutions. Not surprisingly, religion, which is an institution organized around the idea of a super-sensory world, came into being at the same time as writing, and religion consists of imaginary stories. Eventually, humans began to make non-religious stories and to produce them as plays with moral lessons, such as Sophocles' *Oedipus Rex*. Both religion and early literature promoted norms that ensured the survival of human civilization by promoting behavior useful to cooperative communities. From an evolutionary perspective, literature is functional; it assists the learning process that all humans must undergo if complex cooperative human civilizations are to survive.

The trouble is that by now, with so many different human genetic lines splintering within the larger species, no one agrees about what the norms should be. Some humans seem closer to our ancestral past. They fear danger and favor social rules that control others. They value survivalist self-interest and self-assertion over community cooperation amongst equals. They are at home with violence and weapons. Others are less fearful of danger and favor norms that allow others to do as they wish so long as they harm no one. They value community cooperation amongst equals and feel survivalist self-interest is harmful to the community; it should be regulated and restrained for the common good. They dislike violence and weapons. They also generally display higher-order cognitive abilities and favor super-sensory constructs such as the principles of justice that disallow acts of violation such as torture. The first group is at home with torture carried out in self-defense. One group is hopeful for humanity, the other fearful of humanity. It is as if each looks inside itself and projects what it sees onto others. Those whose sensibility is shaped by our ancestral past see predators in others and feel an urge to exercise defensive control over them; those who have evolved more sophisticated and complex cognitive abilities see super-sensory principles at work in the world that can assist humans to make a better world.

A third scientific approach to literature is ecocriticism, which merges literary study with the study of the physical environment. The physical environment if often an important feature of literary works, such as Willa Cather's *My Ántonia*, a novel about immigrants to America who become farmers on the Great Plains. The land in which they live and work is marked with meaning – the tracks of Indian ponies, for examples, from the time when Natives still populated the area. But is also a harsh adversary that defines and limits their existence. For one character, Jim, it is a world to be escaped for university and education, but he retains a strong nostalgic attachment to those "optima dies" or best days of his youth on the farm. For another character, Ántonia, the land is home, and she remains on it, raising a large family. Life on the Plains was harsh, hard, and brutal, and Cather depicts it as a world of tolerable living only after prosperity arrives and the land is transformed into successful farms. The land is an occasion for advancing the conservative ideal that individual hard work in a family framework, not government action, is what brings economic success.

Examples of Scientific Criticism

Let's consider the opening stanzas of a poem by Elizabeth Bishop called "The Moose."

From narrow provinces
of fish and bread and tea,
home of the long tides
where the bay leaves the sea
twice a day and takes
the herrings long rides,

where if the river
enters or retreats
in a wall of brown foam
depends on if it meets
the bay coming in,
the bay not at home;

where, silted red,
sometimes the sun sets
facing a red sea,
and others, veins the flats'
lavender, rich mud
in burning rivulets;

on red, gravelly roads,
down rows of sugar maples,
past clapboard farmhouses

and neat, clapboard churches,
bleached, ridged as clamshells,
past twin silver birches,

through late afternoon
a bus journeys west,
the windshield flashing pink,
pink glancing off of metal,
brushing the dented flank
of blue, beat-up enamel;

down hollows, up rises,
and waits, patient, while
a lone traveller gives
kisses and embraces
to seven relatives
and a collie supervises.*

The poem compares the human and the natural worlds, and it is about death, the passage from animate human life back into inanimate physical existence. The process of thought in the poem's construction enacts that transfer between animate human and inanimate physical worlds in such a way that death seems an acceptable natural process rather than something harsh and harmful that interrupts human life and is entirely alien to that life. The poem is about how life is already natural before death. Bishop gets the idea across by using analogies between human life and the natural world and direct transfers of terms from one domain to another, from natural to human and human to natural.

The primary image scheme in the poem is of a journey that in the "late afternoon" is headed toward death. But it is a journey that is characterized in warm terms rather than cold ones ("kisses and embraces"). The usual fear and anxiety associated with death are absent. The bus journey is associated with family, dog, church, and natural cycles such as a bay coming and going with the tides. Another image scheme present in the poem is inside/outside. Home normally is inside, while the world of nature is outside. But in this poem, home is everywhere and especially in nature. And of course, death is more fearful if it appears to be something outside of us that intrudes into our animate life. Bishop forces us to experience the outside as inside so that nature seems less a separate element of life and more something

* You can find the whole poem at http://www.poets.org/viewmedia.php/prmMID/15213.

that is already inside our life. She lists "fish and bread and tea," and fish here can either be dry or cooked fish eaten at supper with bread and tea, or it can be another characteristic element of "narrow provinces" along with the usual customary practice of having bread with tea in the evening. The fish in the bay are part of narrow provinces in the same way that bread and tea are. The bay coming in or out on the same "rides" that the herring take is converted into an aspect of human life when it is declared to be not "at home." If it is outside human life, it is so only because it is momentarily absent, like someone familiar who has stepped out of the house for a bit. The natural world is also assigned human qualities ("veins"), and human objects are assigned natural qualities ("flank"). The sense of life that Bishop is promoting in the poem is one that requires a different tone and attitude than the usual one regarding death, which often makes us somber and sad. In Bishop's poem, death is mixed in with life, just as the natural world is stitched into the human world. There is no reason for sadness in a world characterized by "hollows" one must descend and "rises" one must climb, the perfectly natural contours of human and natural life that simply must be accepted because they are so natural. And this accounts for the comedic image of the collie who "supervises," a human activity assigned to a dog. If humanity is natural, nature is human in the sense that it is simply another form of animation.

Bishop's poem is about "embodied mind," the fact that all of our thought processes are physical acts in a physical world. She uses several basic conceptual metaphors and image schemes of human thought (in/out, journey/goal, animate/inanimate) to generate her theme that we are part of the world we observe and live in. Our words arise from it, like natural events, and all of our constructs (like churches) are comparable to it ("ridged like clamshells") because they are part of it. They have similar natural shapes and physical proportions to natural objects, and so they can be made into analogies for one another. The way Bishop constructs analogies in the poem is therefore itself reassuring. Like the theme that human life is natural and therefore death is not frightening and should be accepted, the analogies enact the naturalness of human life.

The Scarlet Letter is about a clash of norms between two seemingly very distinct groups within the human species. Whether they are two by now separate genetic lines remains to be seen, but they are remarkably unalike. Hawthorne himself was a liberal Democrat, and he favored the opening of the American economy to all aspirants. The economy needed opening to poor and immigrant groups because it was controlled by men of wealth who belonged to the Whig party and who were largely descended from the first settler group in America. They used the government to further the interests of their own group. Government was used to control private or individual behavior that was at odds with this group's dominant position in society. Proper behavior was for them self-controlled and self-disciplined. Virtue consisted of restraining one's natural urges. Such self-control fostered behavior in the elite that bound them together as a group with shared values and that safeguarded their wealth by ensuring that behavior deleterious to it would be discouraged. If the mass of people were made to submit to the discipline of "moral government," they too would be less likely to take the property of the elite or to rebel against those who dominated the economy of America.

Dominance is a feature of primate behavior. A small group of allies will achieve dominance through violence and intimidation. The purpose of violence and intimidation is control – to make others submit to one's will – and the purpose of such control is control over resources that ensure survival. The Whig party sought dominance politically for a wealthy group that was already dominant economically. And it sought to impose control over others through moral legislation that outlawed such things as adultery. In a post-natural, modern civil world, dominance has to be achieved by non-physical means. Laws against adultery of the kind that hang in the background of *The Scarlet Letter*, which is after all about an illicit sexual affair and its consequences, were important as means of ensuring that the larger and potentially threatening population was self-controlled.

In this framework, the Puritan governors in the novel should be seen as a metaphor for a contemporary dominant social group, the propertied Whig social elite in mid-19th-century America. In American society at the time, new groups, mostly immigrant, were attempting to break in to the closed economy. They could only do so if the ideals Hawthorne advances in the preface to the novel, such as "natural talent," were taken seriously. Hawthorne stresses in the preface that inherited wealth and government-supported economic activity favorable to the elite minority are harmful to society. In the novel he aligns his rebels against dominance, Hester especially, with Catholicism, a religion common to immigrant groups but inimical to the ideals and values of the dominant Protestant group. He emphasizes both her and Arthur Dimmesdale's natural talents and creative abilities. An economy open to talent would allow more people access to resources. The emphasis on creativity in the novel, therefore, is a metaphor for an alternative to the Whig elite's way of conducting life. Hawthorne in the novel is arguing for greater economic fairness and openness in a challenge to the dominant group of his time.

Such arguments are common in human society and usually lead to social conflict. By the end of the 19th century, America would indeed be riven by serious and at times violent conflict between workers and the owners of industry and of capital. Like other primate groups, humans operate with a strong sense of fairness and unfairness. Among primates, when one member of the community sets himself over everyone else and treats others unfairly, a sense of egalitarianism kicks in. Other members of the group band together to attack the dominant one and reduce him or her to being once again their equal. Such egalitarianism also operates in human societies. The seizure of large amounts of resources generates a sense of unfairness fueled by a seemingly innate sense of egalitarianism.

Hawthorne's argument in *The Scarlet Letter* – that the use of moral legislation to control natural urges is wrong – is linked to a larger polemic regarding Whig elite control over resources. Such control, he argues, stifles human talent; it goes against nature. And nature for him and other Democrats was a super-sensory principle in human life that made everyone equal in principle even if they differed in actuality. Such thinking in terms of super-sensory principles permitted liberal Democrats at the time to see things in the world – ideal principles – that their Whig adversaries could not see. A cognitive difference became a political difference. The Whig desire to control resources and to control others to safeguard the control over resources suggests a more ancestral disposition in them, one that probably did not benefit from the adaptation that led to higher-order super-sensory cognition that permitted Democrats like Hawthorne to see principles that ensured fairness in the world. Such thinking is what he celebrates in the preface, when he writes of the romance aesthetic, which "spiritualizes" the world by converting mere facts into embodiments of ideas and ideals. Like many pre-contemporary thinkers and writers, he confused the super-sensory with religious ideas of "spirit," but what he was describing was the realm of super-sensory cognition that seems to be an adaptive feature of some, but not all, humans. Such cognition, as Hawthorne describes it, stands in striking contrast to the Whig cognitive ideal of "common sense," of a form of cognition limited to simple sensory perception that lacks a power of imagination that would permit ideal principles to be conceived. In the novel, then, we see not only a conflict between a group oriented toward resource accumulation and control over others and a group of outsiders arguing for access to resources and an end to control. We also see a difference between two different cognitive abilities, one that can imagine principles and another that has allowed primitive survival instincts to be more paramount because it seems to lack that particular adaptation.

The physical landscape often supplies meaning in literature and film. The forest in *The Scarlet Letter* is an important narrative device because Democrats like Hawthorne believed divinity resided in nature. Therefore, when Hester and Arthur meet in the forest it has the meaning of direct contact with a divine spiritual principle in nature, a principle that assures us that human nature is good and does not need to be controlled by Puritan/ Whig churchmen. Their child Pearl is an index of the goodness of nature. She has not been raised in the church, yet she is characterized by Hawthorne as a direct embodiment of spirit. Moreover, the open land to the west was for Democrats a means of guaranteeing that their economic ideal of equal opportunity for all could be fulfilled. When Hester tells Arthur to flee to the west, it has the added meaning of seeking out the opportunity to survive economically that is not possible on an East Coast whose economy is dominated by the Whig elite.

The novel is often characterized as an entertainment form appropriate for the middle classes, and such people usually do not live in the country. More often than not, they are city or town dwellers. Nevertheless, they, like everyone, inhabit places that have a variety of meanings, from the London underworld of Charles Dickens, which serves the symbolic function of making middle-class values of industry and responsibility seem laudatory, to the troublingly mediocre suburbs of Richard Yates' *Revolutionary Road*, places whose uniformity helped inspire a generation of rebels against conformity. Place is an important aspect of meaning in many works of fiction.

As a visual medium, film often uses landscape and symbolic images of nature to create meaning. One of the first American films, D. W. Griffith's *A Corner in Wheat*, depends on a simple juxtaposition of landscape and business office. A farmer is depicted sowing seeds in images that portray him as in close contact with the natural rhythms of life, while an investor, the "Wheat King," is portrayed in the tight space of an office and in relation to a frenzied commodities trading floor that contrasts with the peaceful, harmonic, and symmetrical images of the farmer in the landscape. The argument of the film is that the contrivances of investment upset the natural processes necessary to keep human life going. The Wheat King's manipulation of the market results in a rise in prices for bread, and the very farmer who raised the wheat for the bread is unable to buy it. Here is the entire short film: http://www.youtube.com/watch?v=PSF7p_DAAxw.

One of the most evocative uses of landscape occurs in John Ford's famous *The Searchers*. A "Western," a genre concerned usually with cowboys and Indians, it tells the story of a man named Ethan who sets out to find a girl kidnapped by Natives. He finally finds her and returns her to her home. Throughout, the landscape acts as a symbol of "wilderness," of all that is opposed to civilization, from the threat of death to a lack of civilized norms regarding property, sexuality, and marriage. Ethan is at first identified with the wilderness: he is a thief; a rebel against government; and he is capable of violence. To save the community where his brother has a farm and a family, Ethan must be capable of acts that are enjoined by the rules of civilization, such as murder. The film argues that those rules prevent civilization from saving itself; it must rely on outsiders who are loyal to civilization but who nonetheless are capable of acting in an uncivilized manner. After the Native attack that kills Ethan's brother and his family, a group of men sets out to search for the kidnapped girls of the family. Initially, the landscape dominates them in the images. They seem small in relation to it. Eventually, under Ethan's leadership, they rise above the landscape, and by the end, Ethan and the other men stand on top of a plateau looking down on the Indian village. The changing relationship to the landscape registers important changes in the story of the film. The dominance of the landscape in the early images is a correlate of the way the absence of norms the Natives represent has come to triumph over the norm-respecting settler community.

Here is the opening image of the movie, which dramatizes the distinction between the landscape and the civil community: http://www.youtube.com/watch?v=Fy2-abqR8B4&feature=related (or search for "The Searchers – 1" on YouTube).

Ethan is associated with two large outcroppings of rock that suggest the natural strength he bears while also suggesting visual order and the possibility that his strength will be a means of bringing order to the world.

In this segment, note how the landscape dominates the searchers: http://www.youtube.com/watch?v=zsXrNXmkB70&feature=related (or search for "The Searchers 2" on YouTube).

Finally, in this segment, near the end of the film, note how the relationship between searchers and landscape has been reversed. They now stand above it: http://www.youtube.com/watch?v=g-r6zOwGjIs&feature=related (or search for "The Searchers 12" on YouTube).

What *The Scarlet Letter* and *The Searchers* suggest is that the physical landscape can be invested with meaning in quite different ways. For Hawthorne, writing in the 1840s, when democratic liberalism was engaging in a critique of moral and economic conservatism, the landscape offered a metaphor for hope, achievement based on talent, and liberation from moral control by those in a position of dominance in society. For the makers of *The Searchers*, working in the conservative 1950s, when the ideal of moral control was being reasserted in conjunction with the suppression by those in a position of dominance of internal dissent, in the name of "anti-communism," the landscape served as a metaphor for the dangers that made moral control and the suppression of dissent seem warranted. What both positions overlook, precisely because they are transforming the landscape into something metaphoric, is the historical landscape and the problem of its previous inhabitants. The settlement of North America was in truth a conquest, and it successfully displaced a Native population. In these works of culture, that displacement is either ignored or else portrayed in heroic terms as a necessary step to quell aberration and abnormality. By becoming figures for White fears, the Natives become more easily victims of White violence.

Things to Look for in Literary and Cultural Texts

- How does the work manifest aspects of human life that are the result of evolution – things such as cognitive ability, adaptive flexibility, functionality, dominance, etc.?

- What does the work reveal of a common human nature that is the product of evolution and that serves an adaptive function in human survival? How does the work display splintering within the human species?

- How does the text show concept schemes at work? What are those schemes? How does the author use metaphors to organize perception and thought?

- What role does the physical landscape play in the work? Are there significant places or locations that organize the experience of the characters or that serve as important markers in their lives?

10

Film Studies

Major Works

D. Bordwell and K. Thompson, *Film Art*
G. Mast, *Film Theory and Criticism*
P. Rosen, *Narrative, Apparatus, Ideology*
J. McCabe, *Feminist Film Studies*
L. Devereaux, ed., *Fields of Vision*
T. Elsaesser, *Film Theory*
M. Ryan, *An Introduction to Film Analysis*

Major Ideas

- Films can be analyzed both as stories, like novels, and as visual objects, like paintings. Narrative films are constructed in the same way as novels through the selection and combination of scenes; the same critical approaches that apply to verbal fiction, such as Formalism and Structuralism or Historical and Psychological Analysis, also apply to film. But as a visual medium, film demands a different set of analytic and critical tools in order to be understood. Films are carefully constructed visual objects, and each element of that construction can function to generate meaning. The primary elements of meaning in film are composition (the arrangement of objects within the visual frame), editing, and art direction, which encompasses everything from color and sound to set and location.

An Introduction to Criticism: Literature / Film / Culture, First Edition. Michael Ryan.
© 2012 Michael Ryan. Published 2012 by Blackwell Publishing Ltd.

- An important element of compositional meaning is the frame. Where the camera is placed in relation to the action determines the size and shape of the frame of the image. Terms like "long," "close," "medium," and "high angle" describe the various possibilities for camera placement. A close shot (one in which the camera is close to the action) generates "tight framing," while a long shot (one in which the camera is distant from the action) generates "loose framing."

- The same kind of image, say a close-up, can vary in use and in meaning. In one film it may signify emotional openness and authenticity; in another, it might signify untrustworthiness, especially if it is combined with other elements of image construction such as dark lighting. Film techniques and the meanings they convey vary according to the context in which they are used. No particular meaning is guaranteed by a particular technique.

- The individual images created by the camera are combined in a narrative chain through editing. Most narrative editing provides "continuity," the smooth flow from one image to another through similitude of setting and action. But editing can also use contrast to create meaning. And sometimes a long editing sequence (a *montage* sequence) can constitute a significant part of a film's narrative.

- The third major element of film meaning – art direction – comprises set design, sound, choice of location, props or significant objects, lighting, and color.

Major Terms

Field of Vision   What one sees from the camera, which is different from the place or setting in which the film story occurs. Related to **depth of field**, the amount of space that is in focus in an image. An object in focus in the deep background of a shot has a more expansive depth of field, while an object in focus closer to a camera has a more shallow depth of field.

Frame/Framing   The border of the image which demarcates the space of the action. The frame also creates the visual space of the image and is an important element of meaning because it selects, limits, and expands what can be seen and what contributes to meaning. Framing can be **loose** or **tight**, distant from the object filmed or close to it.

Mise-en-scène   A French term from theater that refers to the arrangement of elements (characters, props, set, space) within the frame of the image.

Visual Plane   Most shots contain a single visual plane, a point where focus occurs. All in front and all behind is out of focus. Some images in "deep-focus photography" contain several visual planes because focus occurs at two or three different points.

Pro-Filmic Space   The space in front of the camera within the frame of the image.

Shot   Any image filmed with a camera. Shots can be close, medium, long, low-angle, high-angle, crane, dolly, track, handheld, eye-level, pan, tilt, wide-angle, and establishing.

Deep Focus   Deep focus lenses allow for greater depth of field, so that the background and the foreground can be simultaneously in focus.

Projection (Front and Rear)   Filming against a background onto which images are projected.

Zoom   Zooms move from a distance continuously to be close to an object or move from being close to an object to being far from it (**zoom in, zoom out**). This is achieved by changing the focal length of the camera between a wide-angle lens and a telephoto lens.

Continuity   Editing that matches action and objects from one sequence of images to the next so that the story is told continuously and no breaks occur in the visual flow.

Cut   The transition from one shot to the next. Includes **crosscutting** and **inter-cutting**. In crosscutting, two simultaneous and related actions are depicted, and the film cuts back and forth between them – as when in a chase, one character pursues and another is pursued. Inter-cutting is the insertion of a piece of film from another action in the middle of a sequence.

Montage   A dynamic editing style that combines many shots, often rapidly, to make a point (about, say, the passage of time or the evolution of a character).

Reverse-Angle Shot   A shot that reverses the perspective of a preceding shot. Often used in dialog and called **shot reverse shot** to name the switching back and forth between interlocutors.

Diegetic Sound Sound that emerges from the action on the screen. **Nondiegetic sound** does not emerge from the screen action. Often this consists of an orchestral score and is called **background music**. Related is **synchronous** and **nonsynchronous sound**. The first is sound that emerges from the action and accurately represents or matches it. The second is sound that is not matched to the image. Nonsynchronous sound often occurs at **sound bridges** between scenes, when sound from one carries over into another.

High-Key Lighting When light fully illuminates the set, bringing the objects filmed to a brilliant clarity of outline. Related to **low-key lighting** which under-lights a set to create shadows and less clarity of vision.

Three-Point Lighting Used to create a realist effect that eliminates shadows, this technique uses three lights. A **key light** illuminates the characters; a **fill light** eliminates shadows; and a **back light** fills in the space between the characters and the back of the set.

Diegesis The term used to name the story depicted on screen – as opposed to the story in real-life time that the screen narrative is about.

Sequence A part of a film's narrative that records a complete action or event from beginning to end.

Classical Realism The style of filmmaking associated with the Studio system of production in Hollywood from the 1920s through the 1950s. Images were usually crisp and clear, and lighting was designed to create an illusion of perfect realism – the world as seen through a picture window.

Expressionism A style of filmmaking that uses technique in extreme ways to create heightened emotional and psychological effects or to portray the world in a highly evaluative manner. Such filmmaking also depicts inner emotional and psychological states. The style ranges from political films such as *Metropolis*, in which extreme angles and symbolic lighting, enable a critique of capitalism, to moral films such as *Mildred Pierce*, which concern characters that are depicted as innately immoral.

Film Noir Literally, "black film," this kind of art direction emphasizes high contrasts of light and shadow. This style uses a lot of **backlighting** (lights shining on an object from behind it so that it is blackened out).

Neorealism A film style that emphasizes simplicity by using documentary techniques, location shooting rather than expensive studio sets, and usually nonprofessional actors.

Summary and Discussion

Narrative filmmakers tell stories with meaning, much as novel writers do. But filmmaking is different because it is a visual medium that requires very different tools and techniques for creating meaning.

A narrative film begins as a story, but for the story to be realized and turned into a film, a set must be chosen or constructed, and actors must create the characters. The cinematographer then places the camera and chooses the shots. The shots must then be orchestrated in a sequence through editing.

The shot is the basic element of meaning in film. It demarcates what visual space is within the frame of the image. The visual space will be filled with elements that are composed in relation to one another, as in the image in color plate 1 from a 1946 film called *The Best Years of Our Lives*.

Notice how the composition works in terms of both symmetry and asymmetry. Symmetry in this image is created by the visual line that goes from the woman in the foreground, who is handling passengers who want to board a flight, to the soldier leaning on the counter looking at her, to the Black baggage carrier in the background. Why would the director and the cinematographer create such a clear visual line that seems to connect the three different characters? It probably is to make some point about something they have in common. One thing they have in common is that they all wear uniforms. They all serve others in some way.

Now notice the asymmetry in the image. There is a large man standing off to the left. He seems at odds with the other two characters. They form a visual line, while he is outside that line and athwart it. He seems almost opposed to them in that he is on the opposite side of the frame. But how might he be opposed? As the scene unfolds, we learn that the soldier leaning on the counter comes from the working class. He is poor. At this moment in the film, he has just returned from World War II and is trying to get a ride home, but he is not allowed on the plane because he cannot afford a ticket. The large man turns out to be a wealthy businessman, and he is able to pay extra to have his golf clubs put on the plane. The sense of opposition in the visual composition of the image now makes sense. The three uniformed characters are all from the working class. They serve in different ways by carrying bags or fighting wars or selling tickets. So they are aligned visually and in terms of their social standing. The businessman, in contrast, is from the upper class. His wealth places him in opposition to the other three characters. Their interests do not coincide, and that is demonstrated by the fact that the soldier, although he has made sacrifices for the businessman by fighting a war (and giving up "the best years of our lives"), is pushed off the plane in order to make room for the businessman's golf clubs. The film-makers are making a point about the reality of class difference in America in the wake of World War II. The film deals with that problem. It consists of an argument in favor of helping veterans, even if that means sacrifices by the business class. The way this early image in the film is composed sets the stage for that argument.

This image uses a fairly standard medium shot, one that is not that far from the action. The camera is not angled in any way. Angles and camera movement can be used to create meaning and to advance theme. Low angles can either make someone seem important or make them seem arrogant and pompous – depending on the tone of movie. High angles have similar effects, making people seem less important or overpowered or dominated. Notice in color plate 2 that the high angle favors the man standing next to the car. The woman in the car must look up at him, and the image seems to suggest a power relationship between the two in which he is dominant. The film is *The Birds*, and it concerns a woman who is portrayed as being "too independent" and who must be taught to submit to men. The choice of the high-angle shot is therefore an important device for advancing that theme.

Individual shots and single compositions are the basis of film meaning, but film stories are narratives made up of images combined in a sequence that makes sense both as a story and as set of moral, philosophical, ideo-logical, and political themes. Editing used in story-telling usually operates by establishing continuity from one image to the next. Contrasts often are used to interrupt such continuity and to lend meaning to images. For example, color plates 3 and 4 are from a sequence near the beginning of *The Philadelphia Story*. The man is the ex-husband of the younger woman. Her mother and her much younger sister are also in the scene. The husband is a charming ne'er do well who has returned on the day of his ex-wife's wedding to a new husband, and he is determined to win her back. As part of that process, she must change from being an "overly" independent (this is 1941, mind you) woman to a more traditional housewife. Notice how the characters are *blocked* in the first image. The man stands with the mother and the younger sister, and they form a nice, near-symmetrical line. They look in harmony and look like a unified group or community. His ex-wife stands apart, a sign of her independence and strength, but in this image her position also has a negative element to it. She is not part of the nice, symmetrical, harmonious community on the other side of the frame. But in the next image, which occurs later in the same sequence, she has assumed a position with her mother and her sister, and now she looks part of a harmonious and symmetrical community. This second image foreshadows her fate in the film. She will eventually come to accept a more traditional woman's identity, and she will relinquish some of her tough independence and reconcile with her former husband.

Let's now consider a longer editing sequence that makes a point by juxtaposing different images. *Dirty Harry* is a conservative polemic against the liberal Supreme Court decisions of the 1960s that gave greater protection to suspects in criminal cases. Police were now required to inform them of their rights and were enjoined from using force to coerce confessions. Harry is a tough cop who rejects the liberal approach and prefers to use torture when the situation demands. Harry captures a killer who has terrorized the city, but he then learns that the killer will be released because Harry neglected to get a search warrant.

In this sequence (color plates 5–10), he captures Scorpio, who has kidnapped a girl and held her for ransom. Harry knows Scorpio has already killed the girl, but his inept superiors do not believe him. The camera zooms out into a long shot of Harry and Scorpio in a football stadium. The sequence then cuts to Harry looking down on the city. He sees the girl being found dead. Next, we see an office building which turns out to be the Hall of Justice which houses the District Attorney's office. Harry walks down a corridor inside the building, and the side shot seems to depersonalize him and deprive him of the power and authority he has claimed or been assigned in many previous framings. He enters an office, and the continuity editing carries over to the office into which he walks. Women work at typewriters, and one leads him to an inner door. Inside this office, he meets the District Attorney and a judge from Berkeley, who inform him that he has infringed Scorpio's rights and that Scorpio must be set free. Harry angrily inquires about the rights of the dead girl.

Simple montage editing here acquires a great deal of additional force from the polemical nature of the material. The audience knows that Scorpio is guilty, so that we are positioned to favor Harry's response to what seems an irrational liberal legal formalism that would place criminals' rights before victims' lives. The editing also works in favor of Harry, or at least of an argument that would position the audience in Harry's favor. It initially portrays Harry as an avenging angel. The lighting imbues his actions with an aura of virtue, and the space created by the long shot portrays him as someone whose strength is required to push back the ambient darkness of criminal evil. The image of the football field also creates a metaphor: the green grass of the football field comes to be a sign of nature, and nature, the film asserts, is a jungle that requires strong, violent warriors like Harry to whom we should sacrifice our civil or societal rights in return for protection from danger. Such warriors are themselves natural leaders, people whose innate intuitions we should trust because their virtues are inherent rather than learned or assigned from outside by social institutions. Harry is portrayed as a powerful sovereign who looks down from above, a position of protective surveillance, on the city. The sequence becomes more polemical in the next shot of the girl's body being discovered. We see this from Harry's point of view, and we are also positioned more firmly in his ideological perspective. He was right to torture Scorpio, it turns out, because he was in fact a murderer, and Harry might have been able to save the girl's life.

The image of the huge, impersonal office that follows in the editing sequence offers a counterpoint to the image of Harry as a strong individual whose power and effectiveness have been frustrated by liberal bureaucratic rules. It is a metaphor for the impersonal government bureaucracy and the liberal legal rules that restrain the efforts of entrepreneurial individuals like Harry, whose superior insight and hard work the film portrays as society's salvation. In the following images inside the office building, Harry is significantly diminished in stature. The camera shoots across the desks, and because objects in the center background of the widescreen frame shrink in size when the widescreen camera shoots from a slightly lowered angle, Harry seems smaller. This also is a world of women and of women's work that consists of bureaucratic red tape that constrains the conservative male individualist and prevents him from attaining his justified ends. Harry is escorted to the inner office by a woman who takes charge of him. The gendered nature of this act of domination is significant because Harry has no wife, and the implication is that tough police work requires distance from women and the values and psychological principles (especially emotion and empathy) they are associated with in the film's conservative worldview. Another low-angle shot in the image that follows inside the District Attorney's office makes Harry once again seem smaller. His entrepreneurial initiative is about to be blunted by liberal rules, much as he is visually smothered by the ceiling. The doors place him within a regimented color line that is a visual correlate of the deprivation of individuality in the face of the impersonal, regimenting rules of liberal legality. If we did not have the sound, we would know from this visual information alone that his heroic efforts will come to nothing.

The third major element of meaning in film is art direction. Location choice and set design figure prominently in the meanings of most films. In color plate 11, from *Mildred Pierce*, a film noir detective story from just after World War II, the set is designed to suggest entrapment. A man has just had a murder falsely blamed on him, and he is trying to escape both the house in which he is trapped and blame for the murder. The spiral staircase is the perfect element of set design to portray his dilemma. The more he runs, the more deeply he becomes involved, since to flee is to acknowledge blame.

Color and lighting are also used to make meaning. In *The Shining*, red correlates with the human propensity for violence, while blue is linked to our ability to be civil with one another. Through the course of the film, which is set in an isolated vacation resort in the mountains, the caretaker, Jack, goes mad, and eventually he tries to murder his wife, Wendy, and his son, Danny. He becomes possessed by the ghosts that inhabit the resort, but that possession is a metaphor for the way we humans can sink back out of civilization and into animal nature. We can cease to behave in accordance with the norms of civil interaction and become violent with one another. Wendy and Danny are associated with the human ability to control rage and violence. In color plate 12, that sense of self-control is depicted in Wendy Torrance's costume. She wears blue over red. Throughout the film, blue is to be found on characters who are highly civil and who can empathize with and care for others. That mode of behavior is quite different from the violent, mutually predatory behavior associated with animal nature. When Jack goes mad and finally sinks back into that animal nature, his costume changes. He begins to be seen wearing a red jacket over a red shirt (color plate 13), inverting the color distribution found in Wendy and Danny. Red, or animal nature, has won out over blue or civility in his personality. Lighting is an important metaphor in the movie. Bright lights along the top of the frame are a metaphor for "shining," the ability to communicate without words, that is also a metaphor for civility, for the forms of communications between people that build and sustain communities. Bright lights are often juxtaposed to toilets that are a metaphor for the human body and for animal instincts that work against civility. Jack succumbs to those instincts and tries to kill Danny, the embodiment of shining and civility. (See color plates 14 through 17.)

In the same movie, sound figures at certain points in the elaboration of the movie's theme. To signal that the family is now in a more natural situation where natural rules of survival might take prominence over civil norms, a coyote is heard howling during the early inter-titles between segments of the film. Tone of voice is also important for conveying the sense that the family is in jeopardy because the animal within is emerging. When they are riding up into the mountains to the resort where they will stay for the winter, they drive in a small Volkswagen Beetle that looks very precarious in the enormous natural setting, a perfect image for the danger the family is in once it leaves the protection of civil norms and enters nature (color plate 18). In the car, Jack tells Danny the story of the Donner Party, a group of settlers who were obliged to set aside civil norms and resort to cannibalism to survive when they were trapped in a winter snowstorm. Danny says he saw something about it on TV, and Jack replies with a sarcastic snarl, "See, he heard about it on the television!" His tone points to the possibility of violence lurking beneath the surface of his otherwise normal-seeming personality. Later in the film he will burst out in rage at Wendy when he finds her reading his book manuscript. He follows her around a large room like a predator, and as he does so we see blood pouring from elevator doors in an intercut fantasy sequence. Suddenly, we hear Wendy and Jack's voices become distorted as if they were submerged in blood. And indeed, their ability to communicate, which throughout the film is identified with being civil, is suddenly overwhelmed by the possibility of blood violence.

Examples of Film Analysis

Michael Clayton is a study in character, a complex narrative, and a good example of how to use image composition and editing to convey meaning. The story of a lawyer who cleans up legal messes for clients of his firm, the film also deals with corporate corruption. Michael discovers that his friend Arthur was murdered because he was about to reveal that a corporation his firm represents concealed evidence that one of its products poisoned and killed a number of people. His murder is ordered by Karen Crowder, the head of the corporation. Michael is drawn into the case when Arthur, who suffers from mental illness, strips his clothes off in a deposition hearing. He has decided to stop concealing the truth and to stand with the people he supposedly is fighting, the victims of the corporation. Arthur's conversion is coded in religious terms; he is associated with Shiva, the Hindu god of death and rebirth. Arthur is reborn as someone who seeks justice. He is a close friend of Michael's son, and they share an interest in fantasy stories about heroes who quest for justice. Early in the film Michael is portrayed as ignoring that aspect of his son's life, but as the film progresses and as he transforms as a character and moves closer to Arthur, he begins to himself quest for justice, and his son's fantasy book becomes a crucial hiding place for evidence. In the end, he decides to avenge Arthur's death by trapping Karen into a confession and by revealing the evidence of wrongdoing by her corporation.

In a film so concerned with one man's moral decisions, the portrayal of character is a crucial element of meaning-making. The opening sequence portrays the corporate world as cold, anonymous, and overbearing. It is a world in which it is easy to absolve oneself of moral responsibility and to simply go along with what the corporation orders one to do. In one image in this sequence, a janitor is shown in the background, framed by a door. It is significant because Michael refers to himself as a janitor for his firm because he cleans up messes. In a later editing sequence, Michael is portrayed visually in a way similar to the janitor, and this editing sequence repeats several images from the opening one. Here is where to find it in the film using the DVD Player timer: 20.45.00 to 23.00.00 (see color plates 19–22).

The sequence begins with Michael at an auction of a failed business enterprise in which he invested all of his savings. He did it to help his brother, who is an alcoholic. He learns that he still owes quite a bit of money to loan sharks. This places him in a quandary that shapes the moral choices he has to make. Later, he will face a choice between accepting money from his firm, that would pay his debt but would require him to conceal the firm's secrets including the one Arthur discovered, and revealing the wrongdoing. Notice how he and the loan shark are visually portrayed at the start of the sequence. The image is dark, suggesting the immorality Michael has gotten himself involved with. The long shot of the two of them seated at the table also makes Michael seem overwhelmed by his environment, and the image is composed to suggest that Michael is out of place in this world.

As the sequence progresses, Michael is seen walking on the street and then entering the corporate building. This is where some images from the opening sequence repeat. Notice that Michael seems to fit in with the crowd and to not stand out. When he walks into the building, he looks like an ordinary functionary, someone without any distinguishing features. He is one of the anonymous mass. Long shots emphasize his smallness in his world. His life is controlled by others. When he reaches his office, his work begins, and it is fairly tawdry work. He tries to figure out how to get wealthy clients out of trouble they deserve to be in. Notice how he is shown again

Plate 1 *The Best Years of Our Lives.* Produced by Samuel Goldwyn. directed by William Wyler. 1946. An important feature of this image is the symmetry of elements on the right side of the frame (the line formed by the three characters in uniform). That symmetry is contrasted with the large figure of the man in a business suit to the left of the frame.

Plate 2 *The Birds.* Produced and directed by Alfred Hitchcock. 1963. This film favors a male perspective, and the camera often takes the man's side. Notice how this high-angle shot creates a sense of superiority for the man.

Plate 3 *The Philadelphia Story*. Produced by Joseph L. Mankiewicz. Directed by George Cukor. 1940. In this image, a woman is portrayed as out of step with a good symmetrical harmony formed by the man, the mother, and the sister to the left of the frame. The film argues that the woman to the right needs to become less independent. The contrast between the symmetry to the left and her isolation reinforces the idea that she is "outside" the norms of the family.

Plate 4 *The Philadelphia Story*. Produced by Joseph L. Mankiewicz. Directed by George Cukor. 1940. This image from later in the same sequence shows the way forward for the primary female character. She has now moved to the left of the frame and stands within the female group. Notice that her change of place has created a new symmetry and a new sense of harmony. By giving up her independence, she can, the film argues, restore good order to the social world.

Plate 5 *Dirty Harry*. Produced and directed by Don Siegel. 1971. This is the start of a long editing sequence the purpose of which is to portray Detective Harry Callahan as a victim of liberal government bureaucracy. The sequence begins by portraying the positive results of untrammeled individual action. A criminal is caught by Harry, and the image reinforces a sense of his singularity and superiority.

Plate 6 *Dirty Harry*. Produced and directed by Don Siegel. 1971. As the editing sequence proceeds, Harry continues to be portrayed as a lone hero in a dark world. He looks down as the body of a girl the criminal has cruelly murdered is found.

Plate 7 *Dirty Harry*. Produced and directed by Don Siegel. 1971. The audience is positioned to side with Harry and to endorse his individualist methods of policing because they see plainly that the criminal he caught is guilty of a horrible crime.

Plate 8 *Dirty Harry*. Produced and directed by Don Siegel. 1971. Harry drives to the headquarters of the District Attorney to be reprimanded for what he has done, and the image embodies the sense of the federal government as a coldly overpowering and impersonal force. It embodies conservative fears of government bureaucracy as something threatening and faceless, a constraint on heroic individual action.

Plate 9 *Dirty Harry*. Produced and directed by Don Siegel. 1971. A low camera angle makes Harry look small in an office dominated by women.

Plate 10 *Dirty Harry*. Produced and directed by Don Siegel. 1971. Another low angle camera angle makes the District Attorney seem to overpower Harry. The DA tells Harry that the criminal he caught must be set free because Harry did not follow correct police procedure to guarantee that the suspect's rights would be protected.

Plate 11 *Mildred Pierce*. Produced by Jerry Wald. Directed by Michael Curtiz. 1945. A man comes to realize that a friend is trying to blame him for the murder of her husband. His sense of panic and anxiety is rendered by a high-angle shot and by the set design.

Plate 12 *The Shining.* Produced and directed by Stanley Kubrick. 1980. In this film, set design and art direction play a role in articulating meaning. Red and blue vie as emblems of aspects of human life, with red serving as an index of humanity's violent natural side and blue as an index of humanity's capacity for civil behavior. Wendy Torrance is associated with civility, and she wears blue over red, suggesting how she contains and controls natural violence for the sake of caring for and communicating in a civil way with others.

Plate 13 *The Shining.* Produced and directed by Stanley Kubrick. 1980. Jack Torrance is portrayed as perched on the divide between human animality and human civility. Notice how set design is used in this shot to suggest that division. Color is used to portray Jack's move from civility into animality. Notice also in this shot, the first in which he shifts across the line into animality, that he is wearing red over blue, suggesting that animal urges in him are now more powerful than civil restraint.

Plate 14 *The Shining*. Produced and directed by Stanley Kubrick. 1980. Light across the top of the image is a consistent metaphor in the film for "shining," the human ability to communicate and to establish civil connections with other humans. In this sequence early in the film, Jack is portrayed as polite and highly civil. Notice, however, the division in the shot between well-framed blue images on the right and a crazy-looking red image on the left. The blue images suggest the self-control associated with civil behavior while the red image suggests the violent bodily urges that will overwhelm Jack later in the film.

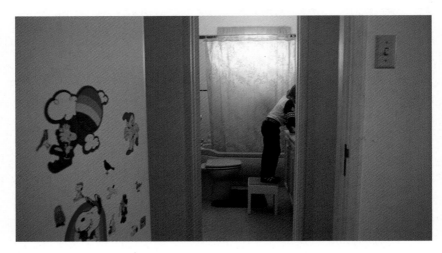

Plate 15 *The Shining*. Produced and directed by Stanley Kubrick. 1980. Upper-frame lighting motifs are often juxtaposed to images of the uncontrollable aspects of bodily life such as toilets.

Plate 16 *The Shining*. Produced and directed by Stanley Kubrick. 1980. Jack Torrance's work room is associated with a dimming of the light of civility.

Plate 17 *The Shining*. Produced and directed by Stanley Kubrick. 1980. Wendy Torrance defends herself against Jack and is linked visually to lights in the upper part of the frame that are metaphors for civility throughout the film.

Plate 18 *The Shining*. Produced and directed by Stanley Kubrick. 1980. The Torrance family is portrayed in tight spaces that suggest how threatened they are by aspects of nature such as human violence. That such violence emerges from within is suggested by the look on Jack's face. He brings the violence of nature into the civil family situation, destroying the bonds that hold humans together in civil association.

Plate 19 *Michael Clayton*. Directed by Tony Gilroy. 2007. In this editing sequence, Michael is portrayed as someone without any moral identity of his own. He is an anonymous worker for a legal corporation who is compared to a janitor and who follows orders and cleans up messes without any consideration for whether what he is doing is good or evil.

Plate 20 *Michael Clayton*. Directed by Tony Gilroy. 2007. As the editing sequence continues, Michael walks back to work from his meeting with the gangster to whom he owes money. He is living an amoral life in which he blindly goes along with the crowd around him in his corrupt workplace. The filmmakers capture that sense of moral anonymity by shooting him in a long shot that depletes his identity and makes him seem part of a larger mass of people.

Plate 21 *Michael Clayton*. Directed by Tony Gilroy. 2007. The editing sequence continues with shots of Michael entering his workplace. These images repeat images from the beginning montage sequence of the film. In this image, Michael stands in exactly the same place as a janitor in that opening sequence. Michael is a metaphoric "janitor" in his job, and as this editing sequence continues, he enters his office and makes numerous phone calls that involve cleaning up other people's personal messes that involve the law.

Plate 22 *Michael Clayton*. Directed by Tony Gilroy. 2007. The editing sequence continues with shots that emphasize the way Michael is part of a technocratic world of impersonal and highly amoral activities that require no one to take responsibility for their actions because they simply go along with corrupt behavior on the part of the corporation for which they work. This image captures the sense that Michael is sacrificing his own moral identity in his work. He looks like someone without any distinct moral personality.

Plate 23 *Michael Clayton*. Directed by Tony Gilroy. 2007. Michael is shot in a number of compositions that suggest a man caught between two visual and moral worlds. In this image, the metal airplane hangar looms over him, suggesting the way his corporation dominates his life, while a more open and clear image of nature beckons to the left of the frame, suggesting the possibility of moral renewal.

Plate 24 *Michael Clayton*. Directed by Tony Gilroy. 2007. Michael's friend Arthur looms over him in this image that suggests how far Michael has to go yet before he attains the same moral stature as Arthur. Notice the contrast in backgrounds. The metal framing above Michael suggests his morally imprisoned status, while the clear wall behind Arthur is suggestive of the clarity of vision he has finally attained.

Plate 25 *Michael Clayton*. Directed by Tony Gilroy. 2007. Michael's moral dilemma is captured in this image, in which he stands between two of his cronies in the law firm holding two documents in his hands. One is a check for $80,000 which, if he accepts it, will oblige him to remain silent about the corruption his friend Arthur has uncovered. The other is the document Arthur was about to release to the world to disclose the malfeasance of the agribusiness company his law firm defends.

Plate 26 *Michael Clayton*. Directed by Tony Gilroy. 2007. Michael walks away from Karen Crowder, having just tricked her into confessing to the murder of his friend Arthur. His size in the frame in comparison to her captures the new sense that he has finally achieved a moral stature similar to that achieved by his dead friend.

from a distance, emphasizing his lack of moral strength. And he is filmed against windows that make his work seem efficient but lifeless, capable but not worthy. He is an amoral person doing amoral things. The images suggest a corporate world where personal values no longer are worth much. They must give way to the imperatives of the firm.

The depiction of Michael as someone who has not lived up to his moral potential is furthered by the way he is filmed in relation to Arthur. A lot of positive religious associations cluster around both Arthur and Michael. Arthur is linked by his name to the Knights of the Round Table, whose quest was to seek the Holy Grail, the container of the blood of Jesus Christ, and he is shown carrying a bag full of loaves of bread, a reference to the Sermon on the Mount, in which Jesus preached that one should stand by the weak, as Arthur chooses to do. When he goes "mad," it quickly becomes evident that he is not mad at all. He is the one who has woken up and become sane. In one crucial scene, he and Michael confront each other in a jail cell. The sequence begins with news arriving at the law firm office that Arthur has stripped his clothes off in a deposition. He is chief litigator in the case involving the cover-up of corporate wrongdoing and the deaths of innocent people. He has finally seen the light and decided to act on behalf of the victims. Michael at the start of the sequence is associated with words like "Jesus," and he is filmed against a background of white and black, an image of the moral choice he will soon have to make. As he walks to the airplane to go to help Arthur and try to clean up the mess Arthur has created, he is depicted with a metallic airplane hangar behind him, but he looks off to the side towards open fields and nature, an image of the world of freedom to which he secretly aspires (color plate 23). Arthur's voiceover dominates the sequence up to this point, and he speaks of his illumination. Michael, in contrast, is depicted getting into a small corporate jet that makes him look trapped in his job. Nevertheless, Arthur articulates hope for him, that he is the "secret hero," just as images of Karen Crowder, the corrupt corporate leader and future murderer of Arthur, are intercut in the sequence. In the jail cell, notice how the two of them are arranged in relation to one another. Michael looks small off to the left lower side of the screen, while Arthur looms over him, lecturing him about morality and ethical choice (color plate 24). Michael supposedly has power at this point and Arthur is supposedly mad, but the visual image says something quite different. It is a good example of visual story-telling (DVD Player counter: 26.23.00 to 30.14).

Michael finds that he finally must choose. Arthur is murdered. Michael discovers why. Arthur had thousands of copies printed of a secret report the corporation suppressed, containing evidence that it knew its product was toxic. In one crucial, scene Michael's moral choice is rendered visually. He stands between his boss and another lawyer in the firm (see color plate 25). In his hands he holds a check that will pay his debts in return for silence and a copy of the damning report. When he chooses to reveal the report and to entrap Karen Crowder, the camera moves out with him as he walks away from her (see color plate 26). She becomes smaller in the frame as he becomes progressively larger. The visual vocabulary now inverts his initial depiction as someone small who is lacking moral substance and is determined by his surroundings.

Things to Look for in Film Texts

- How are the images composed? What are the significant elements within the frame and how are they arranged in relation to one another?

- How is the camera placed, and what significance attaches to each placement? How do the different shots create meaning? How do they portray character dynamics?

- Is the film edited in a way that is important or significant for the elaboration of theme or the construction of character?

- What elements of art direction are important? Is the set or the location significant? Does the set match the issues the film takes up? How is it a comment on those issues? Is sound important in any way? Finally, how are colors used in the film?

11

Cultural Studies

Major Texts

M. Gurevitch et al., *Culture, Society, and the Media*
S. Hall et al., *Policing the Crisis*
S. Hall et al., *Culture, Media, Language*
D. Hebdige, *Sub-Culture: The Meaning of Style*
P. Gilroy, *There Ain't No Black in the Union Jack*
I. Ang, *Watching Dallas*
J. Hermes, *Reading Women's Magazines*
M. Ryan, ed., *Cultural Studies: An Anthology*

Major Ideas

- Cultural Studies brings to everyday life the same tools of analysis one finds in literary study. Advertisements, popular songs, television shows, journalism, gaming – all can be analyzed from a variety of critical perspectives. That is the case because they are imaginative artifacts that bear meaning. They are constructed using techniques similar to those used in film and literature such as narrative, metaphor, irony, framing, and composition.

- As in literature, so in culture, meaning is borne by signs. Signs function because they embody codes (dictionaries of meaning) that are shared by cultural communities. The image on a magazine cover will be meaningful

An Introduction to Criticism: Literature / Film / Culture, First Edition. Michael Ryan.
© 2012 Michael Ryan. Published 2012 by Blackwell Publishing Ltd.

to the community of readers the magazine addresses. Advertisements within the magazine will be composed of meaningful elements that bear concepts and feelings the readership of the magazine will recognize and appreciate. The same is true of the way television shows operate, providing significant narratives that viewers understand because they share the codes upon which the narrative is based. Television detective shows, for example, reinforce a shared understanding of moral order in a civil society.

- Culture consists of texts, institutions, and practices. A popular song is both a text in the traditional literary sense (words on a page) and also a performance, a merger of sound and word that can also, on stage, draw on dance and special effects. The crucial institutions of culture range from public ones such as the BBC or PBS to private ones such as the SONY Corporation, Fox News, the *New York Times*, the Museum of Modern Art, or *Granta*. As practice, culture in everyday life manifests itself in such things as fashion, subcultural style, and slang. Anyone who has done winter sports recently knows there is a difference between the culture of snowboarding and the culture of skiing, with each having a different dress code and a different set of attitudes toward the sport of getting down a snowy mountain fast.

- Cultural Studies began with the study of popular literary forms such as the detective novel, and with such everyday practices as Punk fashion. It remains committed to the examination of the popular realm, but in theory it also encompasses high culture as well and can, in the form of such subdisciplines as Visual Studies, cover a range of high-culture and popular materials. Considered from the point of view of Cultural Studies, the distinction between art and the popular becomes negligible.

- Culture is a realm of power. Those with economic power are able to make cultural products, while those without economic power are obliged to be consumers. Certain realms, such as filmmaking and popular music, are more open to creativity from below on the class ladder, but the production and dissemination of media entertainment requires great resources. A small number of corporations control production in that market. The products they make and promote can be expected to reinforce the values that sustain the economic system in which those media corporations have power. Sometimes governmental power is a factor in cultural production, especially in regard to propaganda. Early Cultural Studies was concerned with the way working-class kids resist domination by mainstream culture. They are channeled toward low-end, low-paying jobs by the educational system, and they are assigned little value in society. Rituals of resistance through cultural practices such as slang, fashion, and dance can be ways to find alternative forms of symbolic value.

Major Terms

Hegemony   The dominant position of a social or economic group can be maintained by soft means rather than by force. In the past, religion was such a means of making sure the minds of those without economic power were trained to accept their subordinate social position.

Encoding/Decoding   The dual process that permits media messages to have ideological meanings for audiences. First, they are created by drawing on established codes of understanding, the assumed consensus of a culture that mandates what will be deemed acceptable thought and speech. Well-trained members of the culture can then decode the messages because they bear within themselves the same codes of understanding that inform the making of the messages.

Subculture   A group within a larger culture that distinguishes itself by some cultural practice that often is at odds with mainstream tastes.

Hybrid/Hybridity   The merging of two distinct cultural elements or forms into one, so that, for example, two styles of music merge to form a new one.

Summary and Discussion

You are immersed in culture and it is immersed in you. Your language is cultural, and within the major language you speak, such as English, you inhabit and speak a local cultural dialect determined by your ethnic background, how much your parents earn, where you were educated, who your friends are, what music you listen to, etc. Whether you swear and use a lot of slang or avoid such things because they are frowned upon by your family and income group is an effect of culture. The thoughts, feelings, and fantasies you have are cultural; they come to you from without and stick to your brain and get turned into you. But you did not invent most of them.

Imagine you were growing up in a successful Nazi Germany, the Third Reich triumphant. Your thoughts and feelings and fantasies would be very different. You would not feel yourself to be a "free" consumer of interesting things like the most recent Lady Gaga album (that would be banned as "decadent" and you would be taught to loathe women who dressed and acted as she does). You would think marching in step a good thing, worshiping great male leaders an even better thing, and hating Jews just plain normal – as normal as detesting "terrorists." If you and your friends like Lady Gaga and would not be caught dead listening to real country (with the exception of Taylor Swift), you are enacting culture. Shop at Urban Outfitters for dark gray hoodies and light blue striped long-sleeve shirts while ordering Birkenstocks for the summer? Welcome to your culture. It is slightly different from the culture of a Hispanic youth in a nearby city who focuses his attention on cars. If you say your school is divided between nerds, jocks, bimbos, emos, and metal rockers, you are noticing that you are immersed in culture and that culture has something profound to do with how we define and constitute and live our "selves."

Not that you do not have choices. But you choose between things given to you by others, often by either a very controlling patriarchal culture in which roles are prescribed (let's say you are growing up in a tribal area of Afghanistan, are a young girl, and are about to be married off at 12 or 13 to a much older man, thus sacrificing all chance of an education or of a role in life other than child-bearing) or by a market-based capitalist culture in which large corporations vie for your consumer money by providing you with cultural entertainment that is designed to be meaningful and attractive to you (the latest X Men movie or the latest Britney Spears album).

But culture is far more than popular entertainment or the languages and taste cultures we inhabit. It is also the ideational world we live in, the world of norms, values, ideals, roles, and the like that shape us from day one of our existence. Culture in this sense enables our lives and provides us with tools for surviving in our world. We learn how to dress "properly," how to behave in accordance with reigning norms, how to speak and even to think in ways that ensure success in life. Within those prescribed patterns and forms, we develop an identity and a way of being that is our life. Not many of us can choose to go off to the mountains and plains of the west and live as trappers, surviving on what we hunt. We can choose to live in an apartment in a city or a house in a suburb (if we are North American), but that depends on how well our culture has equipped us for the work world, for earning a living, and practicing needed skills. Each choice brings with it a different culture.

The culture of suburban life will be very different from the "free young thing" lifestyle of the city. Much more emphasis on child-rearing, for example, and less on hanging out with friends. Less time sipping beer at local hot spots and more spent taking kids to the Y for swimming lessons.

A national, ethnic, or geographic culture can be inflexible and highly prescriptive, but culture also contains multiple possibilities within it for a diverse range of iterations. If you live in the right place, you can pass through several cultures in a single day. Just walk around any cosmopolitan city, and you will encounter diverse cuisines and usually diverse ethnic neighborhoods. In certain falafel shops in Toronto, you walk off the cement and into the Middle East because those serving you clearly are very close still to their native culture and have not adopted the "ways" of western Toronto. But go as far east in Canada as you can go and you will find yourself in Nova Scotia, and you will feel, culturally, as if you've moved fifty years back in time. Things that are considered old-fashioned continue there still. Women still sew and knit as they did in my childhood in Ireland fifty years ago.

Cultural Studies as a discipline began when scholars noticed that "culture" broke down into "cultures" or "subcultures" and that there was often a clash of meaning, practice, and quite often class location between them. When working-class youth developed counter-normative styles of dress and behavior (speech, dance, everyday practice), scholars of culture began to realize that culture could be a symbolic battleground between those with power, resources, and the authority to dictate what counted as normal in a society and those without any of those things. The "norm" and the "normal" can be the expressions of one social group's interests and preferences, but culture is not by any means a one size fits all phenomenon, at least in a capitalist free market democratic setting. Dissonant energies are always at work, especially amongst youth. Add an element of class resentment of the sort one is likely to find in a highly class-conscious culture such as England's, and what emerges is of special significance. Punk rocked, and it rocked not only musically but also socially by questioning the prescribed norms of normality in English society. By inverting the values assigned to certain styles of dress and behavior, Punk troubled the way a culture assigns roles and identities by symbolic means. Those who speak and dress "well" in a business-centered capitalist culture are more likely to "succeed." By deliberately speaking and dressing "badly," Punks refused to accept that cultural norm and questioned the values embedded in it (values having to do with self-control, deference to authority, willingness to accept one's place in a hierarchy, etc.). The novel *Trainspotting* thematized the same "pox on your house" attitude.

The study of culture ranges from anthropology to Media Studies, and can focus on anything from how culture is produced and what industries make it to what television narratives are preferred in which cultural context and how audiences process what they consume. Cultural production focuses on media conglomerates like SONY and Bertelsmann that control a wide range of cultural forms, from television, to magazines, to music. While ownership is not determining of content, under capitalist auspices it is likely that ownership will mean a limit on the range of messages likely to be disseminated. And one can expect that few will challenge the basic economic model to which the media conglomerate is tethered. News Corporation is responsible for the irreverent *Family Guy* comedy series, but it also cancelled the more politically challenging *Firefly* while being responsible for the most explicitly conservative news show on earth, Fox News.

Cultural theorists noticed in the 20th century that high art strove for difference while popular cultural forms thrived on redundancy. Audiences seemed pleased and comforted by predictability and repetition. The same television shows and movies replayed the same basic scenarios of love or adventure. There was little noticeable difference between iterations or examples. This sameness seemed part and parcel with a culture of conformity that policed aberrant behavior that departed from prescribed, often fairly conservative norms. But later empirical studies found that audiences processed culture in interesting ways relating to their location in society. Fan engagement with stars is often highly personal, and the meanings of star culture are not reducible to the model of conformist redundancy alone. Female readers of romance fiction, for example, find ways of dealing with and understanding limits on their lives by reading that fiction. And while popular entertainment often aims for repetition of proven forms, such as genres, there is also evidence of a constant striving for difference and for the new and untried, especially in the realm of television production, where shows such as *Two and a Half Men* are noted for "pushing boundaries" on taste and acceptable subject matter.

While the study of human cultures has long been a concern of anthropology and sociology, Cultural Studies emerged in the literary academy in the wake of the 1960s, and it combined two important intellectual movements of that era – Marxism and Structuralism. Marxists are concerned with class and with the way income differences manifest themselves in culture. They noticed that working-class youth, who are assigned few material resources by a capitalist society, resort to symbolic means of attaining self-identity and a sense of self-worth. Structuralism, the study of human sign systems, aided the Marxist endeavor by providing a vocabulary and a method for analyzing those symbolic activities. Cultural Studies has since expanded to include everything from religion and cyberspace to comic books and pornography. Any symbolic or meaning-laden human activity is cultural and is worthy of study.

Culture is important because it provides us with a vocabulary for thinking about the world we live in. Culture is food for our brains, and it determines how they function. If you watch a lot of crime dramas on television, it is more likely that you will favor capital punishment, for example. Not only will those with a preexisting belief in such punishment have their beliefs reinforced, but also those without preexisting beliefs about the death penalty will be more likely to favor it after watching a lot of crime dramas. Television dramas about moral wrongs tend to instill and reinforce punitive attitudes toward criminals. Similarly, if during the Iraq War you watched Fox News rather than PBS Newshour you would be more likely to underestimate the number of American soldiers killed in the war. Different kinds of culture make our minds run differently. How culture works as a set of languages or discourses that have an impact on how we think and what we believe is therefore an important area of study. It determines how people feel and act in the world. Culture regiments and guides, imposes beliefs and inspires. We see this in extreme cases such as the hypothetical successful Third Reich, but it is harder for us to see it in our own cultural life because we are living it as we think about it. Culture is also the realm where humans are most creative. If values and norms can be prescribed by a culture, cultural work can also challenge and change them.

Examples of Cultural Analysis

The "War on Terror" is a good example of a culturally constructed event. It consisted of both a mobilization of signs that aroused strong popular feelings and an implementation of actions based on the narratives created by those signs that affected people's lives quite directly. It justified an illegal and dubiously motivated war, and it led to the breach of civilized norms such as the international treaty enjoining torture. It left one US President, George W. Bush, so fearful of being charged with crimes against humanity that he cannot travel to Europe for fear of being arrested.

That war began, of course, with the attack by predominantly Saudi Arabian Islamic radicals on the World Trade Center in New York City on September 11, 2001. According to the leader of the attack, Osama Bin Laden, it was motivated by a desire to punish the United States for its support of Israel's occupation of Palestine and for stationing an army in Saudi Arabia, the Islamic Holy Land. Crusaders from western Europe had invaded Islamic lands a thousand years before, and Bin Laden perceived the US presence in the Middle East as a return to Crusader ideology and practices. He saw the US, in other words, through a heavily tinted cultural lens that differed greatly from how the US government perceived its own actions. But equally, the US leaders, including Bush, saw Bin Laden and his movement through a cultural lens that distorted them. Rather than see the Al Qaeda movement as a justified political response to a debatable US action, it saw it instead as a manifestation of "evil," a moral and religious rather than a political category. Such distortions are inevitable because one always sees the world from one's own particular perspective. But in this instance the distortions were informed by cultural narratives and images that made mutually objective perceptions nearly impossible.

Bin Laden murdered 3,000 Americans on September 11, but he himself saw those deaths as a justified response to the 18,000 Palestinian deaths at Israeli hands since Israel was carved out of Palestine in 1948, and to the 20,000 or so Iraqi deaths during the Gulf War, when the US punished Iraq for invading Kuwait and used Saudi Arabia, Bin Laden's native country, as a military staging area. It is difficult to perceive an attack against one as justified or as having a reason, and the American leaders responded to the attack with a predictable refusal to see the larger picture. They declared Bin Laden to be "evil" and invaded Afghanistan, the headquarters of his movement, Al Qaeda. The phrase "larger picture" is interesting because it draws attention to something media scholars study, and that is *framing*. A frame, when placed around an event like 9/11, allows certain information to be noticed and excludes other information that falls outside the frame. Frames promote perceptions and interpretations that favor one party to a conflict while hindering or diminishing the importance of perceptions and interpretations that benefit others. Words with cultural resonance like "evil" and "freedoms" create strong emotional responses that make it more difficult to take an adversary's perspective seriously. American leaders had to choose between applying a limited frame to 9/11 or an expanded one. The limited frame focused attention on the event, isolated it, and did not connect it to other events. That meant it seemed to have no cause, and events that have no cause tend to be irrational. That made it easier to characterize it as "evil" and made it easier for it to be pictured in moral rather than political terms. Moreover, it made it impossible to connect the deaths to other deaths such as those of the Palestinians under Israeli occupation or those of the Iraqi soldiers shot in the back by US airplanes as they retreated from Kuwait in 1991. A larger frame might have made 9/11 seem an act of war provoked by previous acts of war on the part of the US and its allies.

Information is crucial to how we act in our everyday lives, and if we are fortunate enough to be citizens of a democracy, information is all the more crucial since it allows us to assess our elected leaders. Information comes to us from the culture around us, especially from the media – newspapers, magazines, the Internet, television, etc. Media scholars have noticed that journalists rely on official sources for news, and their stories usually avoid contextualization of the sort that would have led them to research, discuss, and focus attention on Bin Laden's motives for the 9/11 attack. The format of journalism focuses on immediate "newsworthy" events, not on the situations that give rise to those events. Moreover, those stories conform to the embedded consensus fostered by official source assumptions. In this case, the 9/11 attack was defined by official government sources as part of a "war to save civilization" and as a "threat to our freedoms." Such a consensus, once established through a cascading activation process that spreads it from the upper tiers of government officialdom down through the elite media to the level of popular discourse, is difficult to challenge. Seymour Hersh and Thomas Friedman, two critically minded journalists, tried to point out that the attackers were predominantly Saudi Arabian rather than Iraqi, but George Bush was a friend and ally of the Saudi royal family while the leader of Iraq, Saddam Hussein, had tried to murder his father, and such a dissonant perspective on the event was not likely to be taken seriously by him. The Friedman/Hersh position was ignored even though it made clear that an invasion of Saudi Arabia would be more warranted than the invasion of Iraq that somewhat illogically emerged from 9/11 as a focus of the American "War on Terror."

The media tend to patrol the boundaries of culture and to keep discord within bounds, and this was a good example of such control for the sake of a consensus initiated by those with political power. Unfortunately, the consensus in this case allowed Bush to engage in an illegal act of war against a country that had nothing to do with 9/11 or with terrorism against the US. The resulting war killed over 100,000 people, far more than were killed in 9/11. And that of course should prompt us as critical cultural analysts to ask if indeed the "War on Terror" was a war to save "civilization" or if it was itself a species of terror by some rather uncivilized people who allowed their self-interest to trump such basic rules of civilization as the one enjoining torture. George Bush instituted a program of torture (in defiance of the Geneva Conventions on War) that resulted in at least one hundred deaths. He is technically a war criminal, although few in the United States would admit that, and that in part has to do with the way torture has become an accepted part of US popular culture in shows like *24*.

The Russian Formalists noted (to return to where we started in this book) that language routinizes our thinking. The simple repetition of verbal formulae limits the range of our thoughts. We become automatons and we more easily submit as a result to something like the hypothetically successful Third Reich alluded to above. We forget that our own seemingly normal reality is not that different. We must accept that the "War on Terror" is a good thing. We can't say without penalty that the real terrorist is George Bush and his ilk. That would be too "extreme." People would stop listening to us because they would think we are abnormal. And of course we would be. We would fall outside the norm established by and expressed in the cultural consensus around the "War on Terror." The Russian Formalists were part of a cultural movement that sought to disturb such norms and sought especially to disturb the way they operated in language. By writing verse in ways that shattered the reigning sense of rationality and logic, they hoped, because they felt language and thought were intimately related, to disturb the kinds of thinking that led people to submit automatically and thoughtlessly to such things as war hysteria, wars on terror, authoritarianism, and the like. From Dada and Surrealism to the Beats and more recent iterations such as free radicals, this strand of culture is as important as the pro-normative function of culture.

Things to Look for in Cultural Texts

- How does the text use signs to create meaning?

- Is the text part of a larger cultural discourse with rules and conventions that shape what it is?

- What if any are the likely effects of the text on audiences? Does it work to convince or to manipulate, to evoke feelings or to instill fear? What seems to be its purpose apart from entertaining?

- How can the cultural text, issue, event, or problem be related to the social world of which it is a part?

Summary: Theory for Beginners

Criticism is something we do with literary and cultural works. But it is not simply a set of tools for use in the classroom or on course papers. It is informed by and it gives rise to insights about our world. Here is a summary of those insights.

1   Culture is nature

Culture only seems to be a realm of images and ideas that is independent of the natural, physical world. Cultural images influence our behavior, ideas change history, and spoken words have force. They can hurt or heal. They are physical things.

Culture is part of human life on earth, a product of our capacities as a particular animal species known as *Homo sapiens*. Most of what we take for granted as human cultural characteristics, such as our pictorial abilities, are only thousands rather than millions of years old, unlike our species itself. So culture and the cognitive abilities that make it possible are a new thing. They came into being a few thousand years ago.

All human abilities are adaptive; that is, they perform a function that ensures survival and reproduction. Evolution works by randomly generating genetic differentiations some of which are retained by natural selection because they improve chances for survival.

What about human culture might be adaptive? Much culture consists of stories we tell each other. Those stories often teach lessons; they store the wisdom of the past and pass it on to the future. They are like educational

An Introduction to Criticism: Literature / Film / Culture, First Edition. Michael Ryan.
© 2012 Michael Ryan. Published 2012 by Blackwell Publishing Ltd.

textbooks, only they are more entertaining. The three movies about the character Jason Bourne teach that it is wrong to turn people into instruments of one's own ends. One should respect them and treat them non-expediently as ends in themselves. In some respects, the movies argue for a very old cultural rule: treat others as you would want to be treated yourself. It might be called the rule of ethical reciprocity, and it is essential that it be widely held if human civilizations are to function properly and to guarantee the survival of their individual members. In human civilization, group survival is the prerequisite of individual survival. So our ability to create a cultural norm such as ethical reciprocity, and our imaginative ability to create stories that communicate that norm widely in the culture can be said to be adaptive. They function to ensure the survival of the larger human group, and that ensures the survival of the individual organism in that group. Because we no longer grow our own food or hunt our own animals for meat, we humans have evolved the ability to attain survival through civil institutions such as money and commerce that guarantee the same ends but by more symbolic and mediated means. For that post-natural civilization to work, however, we must be able to trust one another to behave in certain ways. Laws ensure that, but so do norms that we learn and that aid us in being self-regulating. And culture teaches norms.

2   Words make things

Norms can be universal (treat others as you would like to be treated) or they can be local and specific to a region or to a particular group (respect elders, take your hat off in church, think communally rather than individualistically). Within a society, certain groups can seek to impose norms on everyone else that serve their interest. One of the most persistent problems in human civilization in this regard is the way groups with power (usually because they control resources) seek to promote norms that preserve their power. Often, those norms are opportunistic rather than principled, founded on a specific interest such as increasing a group's wealth rather than on a general interest that benefits all.

Think of the word "terrorism." You probably associate it with violence – say, the attack on the World Trade Center in New York City on September 11, 2001 and with Islamic radicals such as Osama bin Laden. Now compare those associations with this from the website for the charity Islamic Relief: "Islamic Relief strives to alleviate the suffering, hunger, illiteracy and diseases worldwide without regard to color, race or creed and to provide aid in a compassionate and dignified manner. It aims to provide rapid relief in the event of man-made or natural disasters. In addition, it establishes development projects in needy areas to help tackle poverty, illiteracy and disease at a local level."

The world of Islam is clearly as complex as our own, dispersed along a continuum that runs from angry violence to benevolent assistance.

"Terrorism" is a general category rather than a specific thing. It names a type of action rather than one particular action, and it allows us to sum up a mass of things, people, beliefs, actions, events, histories, etc. that may not in themselves be very simple or even congruent with one another in a single simple term. Such a term could never hope to do justice to the complexity of the object it ostensibly names – the varieties of Islam, the causes of Islamic militancy against the US, the ethnic and geographic differentiations within the groups called "terrorist," the multiple historical strands feeding into the present, etc. The word puts that complex reality through a strainer and gives us in the end a singular thing that wrings complexity from the world the word names. It allows us to think and to communicate more efficiently, but it is in a certain sense "false." It does not name a complex reality accurately so much as impose a simple order and a singular categorical identity on that complex reality.

You get a good sense of how complex that reality is when you read about Islamic Relief and what it does in the world. One effect of the word "terrorism" when applied to Muslims is that makes it less likely that you will think of something called Islamic Relief when you think of Islam. (I didn't even know about it myself until I did a web search a moment ago for "Islamic charities.") The constant hammering home of the word "terrorism" in culture means that the complex reality of the Islamic world will be less available to your thoughts and perceptions. You will be more likely to think "terrorism" when you think "Islam" and more likely to think "Islam" when you think "terrorism."

In a sense, words change things by influencing how we know them and what we know about them.

In the 1960s, Michel Foucault (1942–98) studied the way the categories through which we know the world change over time. He concluded that we project order onto the world, and as human culture evolves, the kinds of order we create also change. In the Middle Ages, many people "saw" a natural world that was very different from our own (even though it was physically the same) because they had in their minds categories and beliefs inherited from their culture that influenced and colored how they "saw" or pictured the world in their minds. They saw mere madmen as "saints," for example, much as we see mere Middle Eastern freedom-fighters as "terrorists."

The study of knowledge itself therefore is a useful and important undertaking. It helps to pay attention to the words we use when we know the world. They play a crucial role in determining what we know about the world.

3   We know what we know

When we know the world around us, then, we are constantly imparting to things our own beliefs and assumptions. Knowledge that we already possess informs our perception of the world, shaping the world we know in our minds, lending it a usable unity and imposing order on it that may not in fact be there in the world.

Why do we impose order on the world that is not there? And why do we do so in such a self-interested manner by using terms like "terrorism" that invariably misrepresent the complexity of reality?

At its root, the cause is evolutionary. We must need to do so to better defend ourselves against adversaries in an ancient predatory context, and that adaptive disposition has remained with us.

But whatever the cause, the problem in part has to do with perspective. When we know the world, we do so from a single perspective, and that means we can only know what we can see. Any particular act of knowledge is limited by the reach of its vision. Yet we often behave as if we were capable of absolute knowledge. George W. Bush spoke of "terrorism" as if what he said was true in a full and absolute sense; his was not a partial perspective bedeviled by limitations that make any and all knowledge provisional and partial and incomplete and that make full and certain knowledge difficult to attain. "Terrorism," in his eyes, was what Middle Eastern opponents of the US did, and they did it because they hated American "freedom." That truth was absolute rather than partial or perspectival. It never occurred to him that his picture of the world was determined by his particular perch, his way of seeing from a particular perspective.

But if you switch perspective and ask those opponents of the US why they do what they do, they say it's because the US has stationed an army in Saudi Arabia to protect one family's rule over an oil-rich nation and because the US prevents the world from forcing Israel to give up its illegal annexation of Palestine. But they are "terrorists," right? So they can't be taken seriously. One effect of that word is to discredit their perspective. Knowledge, especially the supposedly legitimate knowledge of those in authority, has a way of enforcing its assumptions, of making seem absolutely true what is merely partial, incomplete, provisional, and perspectival. If other perspectives are given credibility and taken seriously, the stories we tell about the world change.

And some of us, those with power and material interests that need to be served, cannot afford to allow that to happen.

4   Learn Arabic

Because there are multiple perspectives within the world, that world is difficult to know in a full and complete way, and cognitive mastery of the world, such that we can account for everything, is not possible. We would have to become our adversary, assume his point of view, cover all possible perspectives, and relinquish our own natural yearning to have our perspective dominate.

We often react to this uncertainty, incompleteness, and complexity by composing our own sense of order and imposing it on the world. We thereby control the uncertainty of things that arises from the problem of multiple perspectives. We design a category – "terrorism," for example – that we use to sum up a complex reality in a simple, economical, and functional term. It works in our interest and aids our endeavors; it has a use or a function for us. It does not impede our actions by making us think too long and too hard about the world, and it does not oblige us to learn another language (Arabic) or another culture (Islam). Instead, we can ignore those things and substitute a simple image for a complex thing.

What we thereby avoid doing is to assume the perspective of the adversary. That simple mental exercise in reciprocity would disturb our sense of certainty and undermine our feeling of control. It would make complex what is simple, but it would also give us a more accurate and complete picture of the world.

5   Reality is a fabrication

When we order the world with our minds by substituting terms such as "terrorism" for the complex reality of Middle Eastern opposition to US interests, we also help to construct a shared perception of reality that is often at odds with that reality. Humans construct a culture by constituting nations, constructing agreements, forming institutions, designing customs, teaching norms, learning beliefs, and the like. But we also do so by using shared languages to construct a shared sense of what the meaning of the world is. We all know that "terror" is bad, and we forbid ourselves from asking whether it is the result of "blowback," revenge for wrongs done to others by us. If we thought "terror is really justified anger," we would not be able to operate so efficiently in the world. We would have to pause, accept blame, change our ways, and make peace with an adversary we have offended. Those are very difficult things to do in a household, let alone on the world stage. Self-righteousness is so much easier and feels so much better. It is much easier to self-righteously inhabit one's own perspective with full confidence in its rightness, and to act accordingly. As a result, our cognitive constructs, such as the words "terror" and "terrorism," are seen as being indelibly real rather than contingent and made-up, as being objective rather than human-made, as being unquestionably right and just instead of debatable and remediable. We do this both as individuals and as members of a larger culture that, through the media and public discourses such as political speeches, church sermons, radio talk shows, magazine articles, online blogs, and gossip help us to see the world in a particular way.

Your culture instills categories of understanding such as "terror" in your mind that allow you to know the world around you in a way appropriate to the way that world is constructed. You see and know what that world needs you to see and know if it is to remain convincingly "real." When we see the reality of commercial culture, we do not think "This is a camp; we work hard and get life sucked out of us so that a small coterie of wealthy investors can live lives of leisure." Instead, we think "We are all free; we can all consume whatever we want if we work hard to get money to pay for consumer goods." And we spontaneously generate the kind of thinking our world requires of us.

We are offered toys instead of truly free lives. That is what is real, and we can know no other reality. For us, there is no Zion.

To cite a much more extreme example, when good Germans saw Jews being marched off to concentration camps, they "knew" that event as an acceptable part of their reality because they had been instructed to do so. They had categories of understanding injected into their minds by churches, schools, newspapers, and government propaganda that allowed them to "see" Jews as "parasites" deserving of their fate and to "see" German soldier executioners as virtuous "defenders of the homeland." The categories instilled in them by their education within a particular culture – the culture of conservative Nazi Germany with all of its institutions, symbols, ideas, customs, rules, etc. – made them know reality in a particular way. That knowledge then helped to construct the social reality of Nazidom, to maintain in place the institutions that formed it, so that they came to appear not contingent – hence, debatable – but natural, moral, rational, and real.

Our "normal" non-Nazi sense of reality is similarly constructed; we see our world as "real" and acceptable because we have learned categories of knowledge from our culture that instruct us in how to perceive the world.

As in Nazi Germany, our institutions such as prisons, rules of behavior such as laws against theft, and common practices such as incarceration are held in place by well-policed beliefs about what is right and just and what is not. With the appropriate categories and words injected into our minds by schools, families, churches, television pundits, radio talk shows, and parties in power, we cognitively construct pictures of the world in our minds that allow us to live without seeming deviant in our world. If the dominant cultural fabrication has it that all opponents of US interests in the Middle East are "terrorists," we will "see" the world that way. And indeed, it will be dangerous to our health not to. (Try saying "I know some really nice terrorists with good ideas" in your next class discussion.)

A particular fabrication will have become our cognitive reality (and usually our operational reality in the world). Islamic radicals with a justified objection to colonization will have become our Jews, and we will, in consequence, feel little compunction about torturing them. Culture thus helps to manufacture a particular reality. The "real" – that particular cultural construct that we hold in our minds and that is often quite different from physical reality – is of our own making.

6   Not all stories are true

One way that we impose order on a world that may be too complex (too multivariable and multiperspectival) for our cognitive ordering devices is to narrate or to tell stories. We tell ourselves stories that obey a linear order. We make a world of complex impulses, random events, haphazard consequences, and scattered effects into something that seems written by God. First, there was a beginning, and out of this beginning came an evolution, and from this evolving story emerged a clear narrative line that tends toward a conclusion. We like to think those narratives are etched in granite, but it is more the case that they are like lines drawn through the desert that the winds easily disturb and flatten out into something ultimately meaningless and random. We like to believe that our narratives tell true stories about the world, stories in which none of the words used are inaccurate, none debatable, none contingent or changeable in such a way that a completely different picture of reality might have been drawn with a few changes of wording.

In the US, the founding fathers, according to the national narrative upheld by many as absolute and true, established a government devoted to freedom. After the founding of the nation, freedom developed apace, spreading to all aspects of life, moving geographically from east to west. Americans, as a result, are a free people.

But there are historians who tell a different story. They argue that the founders, those most responsible for the Constitution that many see as a counter-revolutionary, rather than a revolutionary, document, because it reduced democracy and increased the power of a monied elite, were largely representative of a creditor class. The bonds they held against the original new government created by the Articles of Confederation would not have been repaid if they had not replaced the existing very democratic government and instituted a strong new national government to overrule the individual state legislatures that were rescinding debt obligations. The detail gets very complex, and this version of events is not characterized by a single thematic idea like "freedom" that transcends the complexity and overrules it, as it were. Like all real history, the story is not that orderly. It notes conflict and struggle, relations of power and domination, dubious motives parading as high ideals, and the like.

Given this contrast between the national narrative focused on "freedom" and what historians think actually happened, imagine two visual images of America's national story. In the first, a wagon train travels in a long slender line straight across a wide prairie toward a golden sunset. Along the way are Indians, Chinese, Africans, and poor Europeans. Those in the wagon train hand out metal tins, like candy boxes, with the word "Freedom" on them. The recipients smile gratefully and wave to the benevolent and wealthy European-descended Americans in the wagon train. When they eat the "Freedom" bonbons inside the tins, they feel a sudden urge to pitch in to help the wealthy Europeans and they begin to push the wagons along.

In the second image, a mob strives all at the same time to climb a hill on top of which is a pot of gold. Only those who get there will be able to afford sustenance and shelter. They claw and fight, and the most powerful push the weaker down. The winners are all European-descended because they band together more successfully. They make sure "others" get pushed back. They get to the top first and, because they are first, they stay there, ringing themselves in, building walls, keeping others out.

The first is America's national narrative. The second story is closer to what actually happened during the first two centuries of the nation's existence. Contemporary critical theory distrusts national narratives of the kind I just described that create a single subject out of complex multi-perspectival situations and a single transcendent theme out of complexly articulated flows of experience.

If you begin with the assumption that all narratives of this kind – national stories especially – are bound to be inaccurate, you will have begun in a good place.

7 Power is belief

Contemporary cultural theory argues that when we believe such national stories, we help those in power to remain in power. And power here is primarily commercial in character; it is not political power, although the two often coincide.

Modern life, at least since the Renaissance in the West, has been organized around commerce. Many assume that the virtue of a particular commercial order goes without saying. Differential rewards are just, social hierarchy acceptable, the unequal distribution of wealth rational. As long as one is a good citizen, a good "bourgeois," all will be well; order will follow from orderly commercial living.

But jails are full of people who disagree, who feel their allotted place at the bottom of the hierarchy is unacceptable and who feel the rules securing the unequal distribution of property are to blame. Because they were not part of the privileged 1 percent who control 25 percent of the wealth, they stole, and in a metaphor appropriate to commercial culture, they "paid the price." But what if they are right? What if the order of commercial culture is simply a rigged game whereby one social group lords it over another for the sake of monopolizing scarce physical resources? That would be to see the simple order of commercial civilization as complex, as made up of relations between terms in an equation such that one's group subtraction is another's addition, one group's wealth another's poverty. It would be to assume the perspective of the adversary, to see the world from different multi-variable points of view and to take their "reality" into account before determining the truth about the cultural world.

Those who control commercial civilization do not do this because if you assume the perspective of the losers in that civilization's economic equation, the rules that govern commercial civilization appear less hard and fast, less secure in their grounding in nature or logic or morality or reason, those axioms (or excuses) that sometimes feel like butterfly wings. It might make less sense that one group should monopolize society's wealth for themselves while another, equally talented but less well-born or well-educated, languish in prison, the victims of poverty. That reality, which everyone who plays by the rules of commercial civilization must accept as legitimate, reasonable, and good, might suddenly appear unacceptable, and the rules that generate that reality as a seemingly unavoidable consequence of a perfectly reasonable economic process might appear debatable and changeable. Or even unethical.

If commercial civilization is a pyramid with a small group of wealthy people at the top, then some force must be at work to ensure that those who are not winners in the game do not revolt and change the pyramid into something more in their interest – a flat rectangle, perhaps. That force is belief. We hear and internalize words like "terrorism" or national narratives like the one above about American "freedom," and as a result, our behavior is guided in such a way that we accept our place on the pyramid, even if we are near the bottom. Those who might possibly revolt do not need to be policed because, in a way, they police themselves. They believe they are free, yet they are modern versions of slaves who are so trustworthy and loyal they are allowed to work without shackles. And that belief ensures they will not take issue with their station in life or the pyramid that assigns them that station.

We willingly bring about our own subordination by learning to be good workers, dutiful citizens, avid consumers, obedient believers, and well-instructed bearers of categories such as "terrorism" and "freedom."

I began by saying we learn norms from culture. I did not say what kinds of norms, or whether they were all necessarily good or bad.

8   You are not who you think you are

Contemporary critical thinking disputes the belief that we are "free" selves whose actions originate in wills over which we exercise complete control. This illusion is specific to a commercial civilization that encourages people to overlook how they are herded and managed and controlled so that their role in sustaining the commercial order by being dutiful and well-behaved workers and consumers can appear freely chosen.

The first challenge to the belief that selves are singular entities in full conscious control of themselves came in 1901, when Sigmund Freud announced the discovery in *The Interpretation of Dreams* of what he called the unconscious. He found upon self-observation that his dreams had motives or causes that came from parts of his mind that seemed hidden from conscious awareness. In those places were tucked away thoughts and feelings that had been pushed out of consciousness because they were too troubling or were inappropriate when considered in the light of social norms regarding morality and behavior. Often they had to do with sexual urges that the culture of Freud's time found unacceptable. They did not match public norms of behavior. You might say that human civilization conspired with human physiology to create the unconscious. All those biological drives that were unacceptable to a particular kind of civilization, one in which sexuality especially had to be controlled so that people would be "good citizens" and "good workers," had to go somewhere. Those urges were part of nature after all and were not about to simply disappear. They were pushed away into a cave in the mind, and we all have one apparently.

Much of our behavior has its origin in the physical world of instinct. We control our instinctual drives in order to be civilized, but they manifest themselves nevertheless in displaced, indirect forms. These manifestations are what psychotherapists call symptoms, pieces of involuntary behavior that are out of our control. They put our unconscious yearnings and fears on display in symbolic form.

Another, later, psychological account of how our minds work suggests we are not fully self-determining selves because each of our selves is constructed in part through interactions or relations with the people with whom we come into contact as we grow up. We "internalize" our relations to others. It is as if we drew pictures inside ourselves based on our interactions with the world around us, and some of the most important interactions occur with parents and caregivers. We draw cave pictures of them on the walls of our consciousness, and as a result they become us, in a sense. Those mental representations help us to form a self, but that self is relational, not singular. We do not form a self and then enter society. Rather, social relations enter us as we grow up and help to form the self.

Sociologists have also studied how "who we are" is determined by "what we are." Our selves are shaped by our location in the socio-economic class system. We may think our preferences are our "own," but many of them replicate those of our fellows in a particular social and economic class location. We absorb taste preferences from our culture, and we mistakenly think they originate with us. Prefer beer and peanuts to brie and chardonnay? Now you know why.

9   You have to learn to be yourself

An important word in cultural theory is performance. Performance refers to theatrical performance but it also has a more social sense. Imagine learning a part in a play. You inhabit the role; you take it on as your own; you perform it. Contemporary cultural theory suggests we do the same thing in ordinary life, especially when we adapt ourselves to the prevalent ideals of masculinity and femininity. We learn to be ourselves by imitating cultural ideals. We perform those models, and we do so at times by responding to our culture's dictates. Our identities are therefore as much instructed and constructed as determined by our biological constitution. The self is not a simple thing that invents its own destiny based on will, pluck, and perseverance. To be "itself," it must dress up, and the wardrobe comes from the cultural world around it. Culture consists of rituals, conventions, styles, and modes which we adopt and to which we adapt as we grow up. Men in the West never wear dresses, but an Indonesian man would not be caught dead without one (known as a sarong; women also wear them).

Not all gender identity is a learned performance, a borrowing from one's culture. Men and women are driven by similar but different genetic programs that are realized through the language of culture. We don't quest for mates because our culture tells us to do so. We do it because our genes won't let us not do it. The fuel is physical but the forms and shapes it takes are culturally coded.

10   Capitalism is bad for you

By capitalism, contemporary theory does not mean the buying and selling of goods. That was going on for ages before capitalism was invented (at the end of the Renaissance in western Europe), and it hasn't harmed anyone so far. But capitalism is different. Capitalism consists of the economic subordination of the majority of the world's population to the will and the power of a minority. The majority works; a minority benefits. That is the essence of capitalism. It is a social and economic system predicated on the sacrifice of the life energies of the many so that a few can accumulate "wealth." And wealth is so valuable because it is power. With it, one can do things others cannot, and one can make happen things that one would not otherwise be able to do.

Wealth is a human fabrication. If you go looking in nature, you will not find "wealth." You will find plants and animals and minerals. And occasionally, one of these such as gold will be branded with the word "wealth" and used in human society to give people the power to buy things from others or to command labor from others.

But gold only has that power because humans agree to assign it value and to call it wealth. By assigning it value, they accord it power.

Value is always a difference in quantity. A piece of paper with 100 on it is worth more than a piece with 10 engraved on it.

If you can figure out a way to collect a lot of the paper with 100 on it, you will be more "wealthy" than someone stuck with a bunch of 10s. You will have comparatively more value in your hands and much more power (to purchase things or to make things happen in the world).

But if something happened to make the paper valueless, you'd have nothing at all. Wealth is that intangible, that much a matter of convention or agreement.

We invent wealth by comparing numbers or by comparing things like gold to numbers, and the numbers only have value because they can be translated into power in a commercial civilization in which certain conventions, beliefs, and agreements about such things as the power and value of numbers hold. The paper in your wallet has a value of one hundred dollars, and the hundred dollars only means something to you if it gives you the power to purchase something else. The amount of "wealth" embodied in the $100 is determined by comparing it with something physical – a certain amount of gold, for example – or with another number – $1 – which represents a much smaller quantity (of wealth and of power) – or with the things you can buy with it.

If I give you less for something and get more for it later, I am by that transaction made more "wealthy." The difference allows me to accumulate numbers of exchangeable pieces of currency. I have more of a particular number (of dollars, say). So wealth is a difference in numbers, and the numbers are usually tokens that contain purchasing power. They are a claim on resources. The numbers and the tokens can be anything – dollars, or pesos, or euros – even shells. What matters is that you can buy things with them or trade them for something else.

The point is to have "more" of something; that is "wealth." It is simple arithmetic. But it is also a differential that assigns power to some and takes it away from others.

Capitalism consists of making wealth for some by convincing a lot of people to work for less than the market value of the goods they make. That way – through the difference between what they pay workers for goods and the amount they make by selling them on the market – the owners of factories or businesses or corporations gain "wealth." Workers have to in a sense be underpaid for capitalism to work. If they received back for their work the exact marketable value of the goods they make, there would be no "profit" and no "wealth."

And what that means is that workers can never become wealthy working, but owners of wealth must do so, or there is no reason at all for engaging in the process.

So if you are a member of the owning class, congratulations. Capitalism is good for you. But if not, capitalism is probably bad for you.

11   Effects are sometimes causes

Because cognition – how we think – is so important a part of our lives, contemporary theory is concerned with mistakes in thinking.

For example, a common thinking error in racist discourse mistakes effects for causes. In the case of African Americans, the effects of past discrimination and enslavement make for a reality of disenchantment among young black males especially. In a world in which the deck is stacked against one, why play by the rules?

But these effects of past discrimination are often mistaken, by conservatives especially, as a cause that justifies new discrimination. The conclusion of this thinking is, "Blacks are disenchanted; therefore, they do not deserve jobs. Discrimination against them is justified."

Social discourses such as conservative racist discourse are the literature of life. They invent our shared experiential reality for us. They teach us how to think, feel, and live. But they can be based on erroneous processes of thought. The most erroneous departs only from the surface of life, the common sense perceptions one has simply by looking at the world. Such common sense perceptions are often mistaken because they stop at the surface of life and do not see the invisible structures and processes that give rise to that perceived reality.

Criticism consists of breaking through the surface of perception and moving past the limits of common sense. It looks more deeply into things. It represents a crisis for common sense perception and belief because it calls its accuracy into question.

12   Identity is difference – and is therefore contingent

One of the most important concepts in contemporary theory is difference. It means that things are interrelated, much as, in an algorithm, one term is defined by another term. What each one is – its identity – is dependent on the other and especially on its significant difference from the other (as, for example, "$x = (y - 3)$").

How might that work in culture?

Let's go back to our initial example – terrorism. What is it? What is its identity such that you know what it is solely in and of itself and you could not confuse it with something else – "freedom," for example, which is often posed as that against which terrorism is directed? According to contemporary theory, terms like terrorism misrepresent reality because reality is too complex to be summed up in a single typological term. The best way to see that misrepresentation at work is to perform a differential analysis. Such an analysis would determine how the thing named by "terrorism" is constituted in its identity by its difference from other things that it is not. How is it made up of relations to other things? How is its identity different?

When asked to define terrorism, most would respond with a differentiation and say that terrorist violence is not legitimate warfare. Terrorists blow themselves up in crowded marketplaces or drive explosive-laden trucks into US army outposts. They do not wear uniforms or play by the rules of war. The identity of terrorism is therefore determined by its difference from the legitimate warfare perpetrated by the US military and its allies in the Middle East.

Now, let's take a different difference into account – that created by the adversary's perspective. How does that perspective see the same events differently? It would justify its opposition to the US invasion of Iraq by saying that invasion was carried out in defiance of international law. The invasion was as illegitimate as any "terrorist" bombing in Baghdad. It might even be called an act of terrorism because many civilians were killed during the illegal invasion. The very presence of US soldiers in Iraq, uniforms or no uniforms, rules of war or no rules of war, is therefore outside the bounds of the norm that distinguishes good war from terrorism – just like the "terrorist acts" against which the US army's legitimacy is defined from the American perspective. Moreover, the origin of terrorism before the invasion of Iraq was the Israeli occupation of Palestine, itself an illegal act of colonization. When the Israelis invaded Gaza, part of Palestine, they committed war crimes such as killing 400 children.

The point contemporary theory makes is that the world is a complex network of events, actions, things, and people. Things in the human cultural world rarely have the consistency of simple identities that are unmixed with anything else. That is especially true of political acts such as setting off an explosive device designed to kill people – be they in uniform or not. Such actions are usually reactions to other actions. They are by definition things connected to other things. They do not possess non-differential or non-relational "identities," nor are they simple things deserving of a simple name. They are complex, and their identity is contingent or relational. Their identity is dependent on relations to other things, and their meaning is dependent on the perspective from which their identity is constructed or seen.

We use words to assign names to things, events, and people. We divide the complex, non-simple, heterogeneous mass of events and experiences up into parts, and we parcel them so that they appear to be separate and unconnected. They come to appear to have separate identities, to be unmixed with anything else. Even acts that are against someone else are as a result turned into acts in themselves – "terrorism" and not "violent response to the American intrusion on the side of Israel and the Saud family in Middle East politics."

Because things relate in an essential way to other things, however, because they are connected, you can't separate them into neat identities that serve one's self-interested purposes for long without the contingency, the insubstantiality and impermanence, of those acts of identity-making becoming evident. It is better to do what contemporary theory advocates – engage in complex thinking that is differential and relational, that takes multiple perspectives and variables into account, that assumes the fallibility of all typological categories such as "terrorism," and that does not take for granted that the identities discourse makes of the world are actually in the world in the same simple form they possess in cultural discourse or in human cognition.

13   We all live in the past

Another reason it is hard to name things accurately is history. Most things are the end result of previous events, and they often are more like echoes than things. But the things or events that initiated the echo are no longer there for us to see; we have to imagine them – another reason why thinking in terms only of "common sense," of what is before your eyes, is a bad idea. A full picture of the contemporary Middle East would require taking the Balfour Declaration into account. But few of you have probably ever heard of it. And fewer know that it was written as a favor to a man who had invented a way to keep gunpowder dry.

History is as complex as our present moment in time. Yet that complexity is often replaced with sentimental Hallmark card images – "Washington Crossing the Delaware," "Lincoln Freeing the Slaves," "Communism Defeated by Freedom," "Iraq Liberated by US," etc. Complex history is replaced by very simple history.

In simple history "terrorism" is an assault on American values. Terrorism sprang up in history unannounced just a few years ago. It is not an echo of a prior event, a reaction to something else. It is not complex, relational, and differential. In fact, it has no history.

But of course terrorism has its roots, and an archeology could be performed of how it came about, starting with the conservative-controlled US Central Intelligence Agency's decision to overthrow a liberal democratic government in Iran in 1953 in order to prevent the nation's oil riches from being nationalized. Or one could go back further, to the British decision in the Balfour Declaration to award part of Palestine to Zionists who then built Israel, which then colonized the rest of Palestine. History lingers in the present, and acts of violence usually spring from prior acts of violence. The best way to avoid responsibility for one's role in that violence is to ignore the chain of relations, of echoes and effects, that give rise to the present situation we live in.

One focuses instead on the present. This explains why those with the greatest stake in forgetting the past are usually common sense empiricists who hate theory. They think only what is present before one's eyes counts as real and only the present is real. In this way, a country like the US, rather than remember its past or picture itself as the provoker of violence, portrays itself as the victim of violence. (Watch the first half-hour of the film *Iron Man* to get a sense of this.) Such thinking would have us disconnect the present from the past and say that no archeology can be performed to show how the present derives from the past or rests on its ruins.

14   The world is all there is

The kind of thinking that contemporary theory seeks to remedy is not so much erroneous as not complex enough. At times, it is overly empirical, at times overly speculative.

In its empirical mode, it thinks the world is made of simple things that have no connections between them. A bombing by "terrorists" in Baghdad is not connected to a bombing by "the US Air Force" in Afghanistan. Yet they are connected even if the connections are invisible, buried in the past or hidden from view. You just need to be able to see a certain way (to theorize, if you will, a certain way) to make the connection.

At times, the thinking that contemporary theory seeks to remedy is overly speculative. Instead of concentrating on empirical things, the real world of events, people, and objects, it imagines that these things are the expression of spirit, a kind of imaginary ether that glows in the dark, magically manages to be unobservable, and nevertheless determines everything like some great, all-powerful, ultimate cause.

But the world is all there is.

15   Nature is culture

What literature does – evoke realities with metaphors, recount stories from particular points of view, construct sequential narratives that create a sense of moral order, and the like – also occurs in the cultural, social, political, and economic world around us. Literature is not just about human social life; it provides us with a way of understanding how our social life works. The same evolved and adaptive cognitive processes that allow humans to organize social life in particular ways are at work in the construction of literary and cultural narratives.

For example, the organization of economic life is a narrative in that it is constructed around a particular point of view, and the story it enacts – the particular sequence of events that point of view brings about or programs – follows a particular pattern that embodies the interests of those inhabiting that point of view. Within the narrative of capitalism, economic life unfolds as a sequential series of events that are logical, rational, and morally right within the framework of rules and norms that are the axioms of commercial civilization. The point of view from which economic life is organized is that of the investor class, those with the "wealth" to make economic activity happen. They set going a particular economic narrative, one in which money lent to enterprises produces work under certain conditions (wages as low as possible) so that certain results can ensue (return on investment as high as possible). The rational norms of the process dictate that gain for investors is good and loss bad, and if workers' irrationally high wages bring about loss, they are bad, not good. This is, after all, a story with a moral.

But a change in point of view, the perspective from which the story is told, would bring about a quite different real-world narrative. If the unfolding in time of the economic process were told or executed from the point of view of workers, the axioms that define loss and gain would have to change. Now, low wages would be seen as bad, and the argument that justifies the extraction of "wealth" would appear unreasonable and unfair. A different moral story would result. Profitable gain at the expense of underpaid workers would be bad, not good. What is good in one narrative frame becomes bad in another. The narrative of economic life is thus "contingent." It depends on what frame is used, what perspective, to get the story going and to make it work.

Human social life consists of a choice of narratives for living, with "narratives" being understood here as an actual life experience spread over time and guided by cultural stories that justify it to participants. Both the cultural and the real-world narrative can change depending on the perspective from which it is told or executed, the axioms that guide it and determine the values at work in its functioning, and the rules of operation that shape outcomes and results. Both the real and the cultural narratives use frames to exclude norm-dissonant perspectives, axioms, and values and to ensure that the meanings that support the continuity and the homogeneity of the lived process are stable, predictable, and enforced. For example, if you are a capitalist, you can't afford to think that the purpose of economic life should be to enrich workers. That is not what capitalism "means" at all.

This explains why the dominant stories that organize the media, government, and education, in the United States at least, the current headquarters of commercial civilization, are all "told" from the point of view of the investor class. To switch perspectives would be to upset not just a social order but also an entire cognitive order, an entire way of knowing and believing in the world. The narratives of the media cohere with the narrative that is economic life by calling "growth," the successful extraction of value from workers, "good." A particular way of knowing and narrating the world sustains the narrative of social life, the actual sequential process of successful value extraction and "wealth creation."

Who tells the stories in the culture thus largely shapes how that cultural world will be organized. Stories are thus more important than you think. Stories are what people believe and how they believe, and how people believe determines how they act and how they live.

That may account for why artists and writers are often the first targets of authoritarian regimes bent on imposing their will on and inducing conformity in populations. Artists and writers often see beyond the erroneous perceptions that conformity to authoritarianism or to injustice requires, and they often imagine alternatives. Cultural stories provide us with norms but they also help us to evolve new ones and to outgrow old ones that have lost their usefulness. Because words and stories are such powerful cultural instruments, they can change that world by changing how people think, perceive, believe, and act. The analysis of the work they perform is thus an important endeavor. And that is what criticism is all about.

Index

An Introduction to Criticism: Literature / Film / Culture, First Edition. Michael Ryan.
© 2012 Michael Ryan. Published 2012 by Blackwell Publishing Ltd.